SINGAPORE CELEBRATE
Legend of

DESIGNED BY ALBERT SQUILLACE

BY RICK HAMLIN   FOREWORD BY BOB HOPE

TOURNAMENT OF ROSES

A 100 YEAR CELEBRATION

McGraw-Hill Book Company

NEW YORK   ST. LOUIS   SAN FRANCISCO
AUCKLAND   BOGOTÁ   HAMBURG   LONDON
MADRID   MILAN   MEXICO   MONTREAL
NEW DELHI   PANAMA   PARIS   SÃO PAULO
SINGAPORE   SYDNEY   TOKYO   TORONTO

For Grampy, Dad, and Diane,
and all the "Men and Women in White."

Acknowledgments

In my research I referred often to the newspapers and magazines that have covered 100 years of Tournaments of Roses, especially the *Pasadena Star-News*, the *Los Angeles Times*, and *Sports Illustrated*. Several books were extremely helpful for their detailed description of past Rose Bowl games, notably Allison Danzig's *The History of American Football* (1956), Joe Hendrickson and Maxwell Stiles' *The Tournament of Roses* (1971), John D. McCallum's *Pac-10 Football* (1982), Herb Michelson and Dave Newhouse's *Rose Bowl Football Since 1902* (1977), Richard Whittingham's *Saturday Afternoon* (1985), and Kenneth L. Wilson and Jerry Brondfield's *The Big Ten* (1967). For background on Pasadena I was grateful for: the Pasadena Oral History Project's *Talking About Pasadena* (1986), Ann Sheid's *Pasadena: Crown of the Valley* (1986), and Kevin Starr's *Inventing the Dream* (1985). Both former executive director of the Pac-10 Wiles Hallock and former rose Queen Margaret Huntley Main kindly shared portions of their as yet unpublished manuscripts. Oral histories from several "Men in White"—Stanley K. Brown, C. Lewis Edwards, Lathrop King Leishamn, and Elmer Wilson—were made available through the Pasadena Oral History Foundation under the direction of Brooke Garlock.

Of course, the Tournament provided crucial guidance and assistance, I'd especially like to thank Bill Flinn, Frosty Foster, Jack French, Kristin Mabry, and Gloria Meade. Other organizations that furnished information and help were: American Honda, the American Institute of CPAs, Berkhemer and Kline, the Big Ten Club of Southern California, the Good Sam Club, Eastman Kodak, Farmer's Insurance, the Flower Council of Holland, Lawry's Prime Rib, Jet Propulsion Laboratory, the City of Pasadena, the Pasadena Police Department, the Pasadena Visitors Bureau, and Videospec.

I'd also like to thank all those people who answered my many questions: Don Anderson, Peter Apanel, Margaret Arnold, Dick Auerbach, Dr. Arthur Bartner, Eric Becher, Del Beckhart, Bill Bell, Don Bent, Jack Biggar, Bill Bissell, James Boyle Jr., Jack Brown, Charles Bullard, Jim Callens, Rick Chapman, Ann Colborn, Dr. David Coleman, Michael K. Conley, Dorothy Edwards Conlon, Bill Corbett, Harry Coyle, Harriman Cronk, Bill Dannhauser, Millard Davidson, Buzz Davis, Norbert Dean, Vern Diamond, Dr. Paul Droste, Bryant Duffy, Don Dustin, Scott Emery, Bob Evendon, Don Fedde, Dr. Robert Fleming, Richard Frank, Susie Gillaspie, Lotsie Busch Giersch, Suzy Hamblen, Monica Hart, James Hile, Walter Hubert, Fred Johnson, Timothy Johnson, Morgan Jones, Jennifer Judkins, Rick Justis, Leslie Kawai, Lieut. Roger Kelly, Glenn Knapp, Margarethe Bertelson Knoblock, Charles Kober, Bill Krueger, Bill Lawson, Lay Leishman, Mary Lejeune, Pat Lejeune, Lou Lujohn, Bill Lofthouse, Margaret Huntley Main, Harold Mauro, Montie Montana, Michael Nakasone, John O'Donnell, Jon Pawley, Jim Peaco, Keith Peterson, Dick Pittinger, Katie Potthast, George Putnam, Dick Ratliff, Homer Renfrew, Aimee Richelieu, Raul Rodriguez, Richard Seekins, Mike Shudinis, Doug Single, Fred Soldwedel, Donna Soldwedel, Beverly Stansbury, Harry Stillwell, Bill Symes, Jack Tallon, David Thielman, Willie Toshiki, Chris Voelz, Bill Wallack, Jim Whitecloud, Dr. John Woods, Carl Wopschall, and Sue Cary Zens.

Finally, this book wouldn't have happened without Jeffrey Simpson's enthusiasm, Gudrun Buettner and Susan Costello's interest, Edward Grinnan's helpful advice, Bill Flinn's determination, my agent Lynn Seligman's persistence, and my wife Carol's careful editing. Thanks.

Prepared and produced by Sammis Publishing, Inc. and
Layla Productions, Inc.
Art Director: Albert Squillace
Assistant Art Director: Chani Yammer

Typesetting by Midatlantic Photocomposition, Baltimore, Md.
Printed and bound by W.A. Krueger, New Berlin, WI.

LIBRARY OF CONGRESS CATALOGING IN PUBLICATION DATA

Hamlin, Rick.
  The tournament of roses.

  1. Tournament of Roses, Pasadena, Calif. 2. Parades—California—Pasadena. 3. Pasadena (Calif.)—Social life and customs. I. Title.
GT4011.P37H36   1988   791'.6   88-13153
ISBN 0-07-025794-9

CONTENTS

FOREWORD

For the past 100 years, the city of Pasadena, California has welcomed in the New Year with the Tournament of Roses Parade and Rose Bowl Game. What began as a small community festival has become a worldwide tradition enjoyed by more than 350 million people in 40 countries each year.

It's a tradition of magnificent floral floats, marching bands, talented equestrians, and exciting sports action, and a message of beauty and peace to the entire world.

As Grand Marshal of the Tournament of Roses in 1947 and again in 1969, I had a first-hand look at the tradition and pageantry that make up this very special event. You are about to have this same opportunity. Rick Hamlin, the author of this book, grew up as part of the Tournament Family—his father served as the organization's President in 1983—and he's given you a front-row seat for all the action.

The Tournament of Roses has truly become America's New Year Celebration, and I know we all have a lot to look forward to as the Tournament enters its second century.

BOB HOPE

PART
1

THE PARADE

1·CALIFORNIA DREAMIN'

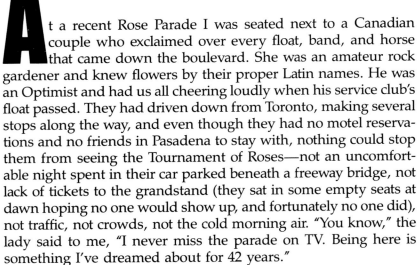

At a recent Rose Parade I was seated next to a Canadian couple who exclaimed over every float, band, and horse that came down the boulevard. She was an amateur rock gardener and knew flowers by their proper Latin names. He was an Optimist and had us all cheering loudly when his service club's float passed. They had driven down from Toronto, making several stops along the way, and even though they had no motel reservations and no friends in Pasadena to stay with, nothing could stop them from seeing the Tournament of Roses—not an uncomfortable night spent in their car parked beneath a freeway bridge, not lack of tickets to the grandstand (they sat in some empty seats at dawn hoping no one would show up, and fortunately no one did), not traffic, not crowds, not the cold morning air. "You know," the lady said to me, "I never miss the parade on TV. Being here is something I've dreamed about for 42 years."

For some, seeing the parade is a dream come true; for others, marching in it is; or for a lucky few, it's being the Queen of the Tournament of Roses. For Richard Seekins, who watched the Tournament on TV as a boy back in frigid Rochester, N.Y., the dream was a chance to work on the floats. Now, he selects the flowers for one of the parade's float builders. For cheerleaders and song girls, it's an opportunity to support their teams in the Granddaddy of Them All. For the players themselves, it's the reward for a successful season. Even for the volunteers who organize the event, working on it is something they have hoped to do— sometimes for as long as they can remember.

Since the Tournament represents all those dreams come true, it's no surprise that its setting is also the scene of many a California dream. Pasadena, known for its old ladies in tennis shoes and the Jet Propulsion Laboratory, for its faded elegance and funky charm, for Caltech, the Pasadena Playhouse, and for a bowl-shaped stadium, set in a natural depression like the Greek and Roman amphitheaters of old, is the home of social aspirations, scientific pursuits, aesthetic achievements, and cultural ambitions. It has been called "the Mediterranean of the West" for its climate, "the Brooklyn of the West" for its many churches, "the Mecca of the World" in a fit of chauvinistic pride, and "the Crown City," out of "Crown of the Valley," which is what "Pasadena" means in Chippewa. Right from the beginning, a uniquely Californian dream drew settlers to her.

In 1873, after an unusually severe winter, a group of Indiana farmers decided to move out to California, choosing the site of Pasadena for their agricultural cooperative. It was not

simply the climate that appealed to them. They were attracted to the possibility of a more leisurely style of farming. They had heard that in this part of the world the citrus fruit just dropped from the trees, and the grapes hardly had to be picked for the harvest. Water, that elusive element, ran in torrential underground streams just below the surface. Here it would be possible to raise oranges, figs, lemons, peaches, plums, grapes, even wheat and corn twelve months of the year, effortlessly. This was the land of leisure.

These optimistic agriculturists were immediately followed by invalids: tubercular victims, sufferers of all sorts of bronchial ailments, neurasthenics, and dyspeptics. They gravitated to this spot, "the sun valley of the San Gabriels," as naturalist John Muir called it, "one of the bright spots to be found in all our bright land, and most of its brightness is wildness—wild south sunshine in a basin rimmed with mountains and hills." They took the air on wide verandahs, admiring the views of snowcapped mountains above newly planted orange groves. As their health improved, they went hiking, hunting, horseback riding, deep-sea fishing. They built tennis courts and golf clubs, and practiced the sort of vigorous retirement that has become the goal of all Sun-Belted Americans.

As newcomers increased with the arrival of the railroad in

the 1880s, Pasadena became the setting for one of California's perpetual dreams—real estate speculation. Large parcels of land were subdivided and the value of lots doubled and tripled, sometimes in a matter of weeks. Even John Muir, as he said, was "sorely tempted . . . to invest in an orange patch myself." The foreseeable bust followed, but not without some developers pocketing sizable sums and erecting handsome palaces on South Orange Grove Boulevard.

This was the dawn of another era, one that lasted for over fifty years: Pasadena as playground for the very rich, a place for the retired manufacturers of Cleveland, Erie, and East St. Louis to enjoy their hard-won gains, a winter vacationland of palms, lawn bowling, herbaceous borders, church on Sunday, and afternoons of croquet. With imaginations unleashed from the often Puritanical restraints of their hometowns, they built ornate Moorish castles, Italian villas, Swiss chalets, French manors, and Tudoresque estates. Resort hotels went up, designed to attract wellheeled winter tourists with the latest in creature comforts. The Raymond opened in 1886 with the then unheard of ratio of one bathroom and water closet for every five rooms. In 1906, the Huntington proudly advertised its two-story garage, "the largest on the coast," with spaces for 150 "motor cars" and 40 sleeping rooms for chauffeurs above.

23

Right: The Tournament of Roses was originally quite a bit more than a parade and football game, as can be seen from the first tournament's list of events.
Below: The lavish Huntington Hotel, which boasted the largest garage on the coast, including 40 rooms for chauffeurs alone.
Opposite top: The first prize-winning carriage, entered by Virginia P. Rowland.
Opposite bottom: The backyard of the Adolphus Busch home became the first Busch Gardens.

Tournament of Roses.

1. Men's Foot Race—1 mile.

R. Collingwood.	A. G. Buchanan.
H. R. Hertel.	Chas. W. Bell.
J. Welsh.	Chas. V. Howard.
J. W. Lancaster.	

First Prize—Pickwick Club Cup, to be won twice.

2. Boys' Foot Race—15 years and under.

F. W. Roche.   Walter Taylor.   Arthur Wilson.

3. Men's Foot Race—220 yards.

R. Collingwood.	H. R. Hertel.
A. G. Buchanan.	Chas. W. Bell.
J. Welsh.	J. W. Lancaster.
Chas. V. Howard.	

First Prize—Pickwick Club Cup, to be won twice.

4. Hurdle Race—120 yards.

R. Collingwood.	Chas. W. Bell.
A. G. Buchanan.	J. W. Lancaster.

5. Orange Race.

R. Collingwood.	Dr. A. E. Nichols.
Ray Conger.	Fred Roche.

6. Bicycle Race.

J. W. Lancaster.	Ed. Buckius.
Geo. H. Frost.	Ernest Conger.
Geo. Simpson.	Theodore Simpson.

First Prize—Gold Medal.
Second Prize—Cyclometer.

7. Boys' Foot Race—18 years.

W. H. Linne.	E. H. Graham.
W. M. Graham.	Raymond Allen.
Frank Robinson.	

First Prize—Silver Match Box.
Second Prize—Handsome Pocket Book.
Third Prize—Pair Dress Suspenders.

8. Boys' Pony Race—¼ mile.

NAME.	HORSE.	ROSE.
Clayton Raymond.	"Elsie."	Duchess de Brabant.
Mr. Scudder.	"Tom Thumb."	"Blackberry.
A. B. Anderson.	"Fairy."	The Bride.

First Prize—Silver Watch.
Second Prize—Full set of Dickens' works.

9. Burro Race—¼ mile.

Geo. Hamilton	"Push Me."
Clayton Raymond	"Slow Go."
And Others.	

First Prize—Engraving, "Too Late."
Second Prize—Saddle.
Third Prize—Pair Spurs.

10. Girls' Pony Race.

NAME.	PONY.	ROSE.
Mamie G. Pierce.	"Bob."	Marechal Neil.
Unknown.	"Los Angeles."	Niphitos.
Unknown.	"Lady Godiva."	Princess Beatrice.

First Prize—Handsome Brooch, presented by Mrs. A. B. Anderson.
Second Prize—Riding Whip.
Third Prize—Silver Pin, Mexican Filligree.

11. Flat Bronco Race—½ mile.

NAME.	HORSE.	ROSE.
C. A. Scharff.	"Fannie."	Meteor.
A. B. Wilgus.	"Small Hopes."	Raymond Beauty.
John Larkin.	"Chopita."	Safrano.
Walter Volkmar.	"Great Hopes."	La France.
Wiley & Greely.	"Comet."	Homer.
Edwin Seller.	"Sunny Slope."	Marechal Niel.
Master Vore.	"Minnie."	Moss Rose.
Frank W. Hall.	"Ramona."	Perle des Jardin.
Frank Simons.	"Bronco Jim."	Paul Neyron.
Arturo Bandini.	"Dimple."	Gloire Dijon.
W. Elliot.	"Rory O'Neil."	Banksia.
D. Russell.	"Brandy."	Hebe.
E. T. Howe.	"Egypt."	Sunset.

First Prize—Riding Saddle.
Second Prize—Bronze Clock.
Third Prize—Riding Bridle.

12. Polo Game—on Burros.

PASADENA VS. RAYMOND.

13. Flat Race—½ mile.

NAME.	HORSE.	ROSE.
Arturo Bandini.	"Dimple"	Gloire Dijon.
W. Elliot.	"Rory O'Neil."	Banksia.
A. B. Anderson.	"Gray Friar."	Gen'l de Tartras.
A. B. Anderson.	"Fire Fly."	A la Marc.
W. H. Syme.	"Claybank."	Gold of Ophir.
O. Stewart Taylor.	"Welcome."	Mad. Welch.
Mr. Crowell.	"Susie M."	Miss Garfield.
F. Simons.	"Bronco Jim."	Paul Neyron.
W. U. Masters.	"Bob."	Empress Du Marcoe.

First Prize—Los Angeles Times Cup.
Second Prize—Cooling Blanket.

14. Hurdle Race—½ mile, over 6 Hurdles.

NAME.	HORSE.	ROSE.
W. U. Masters.	"Bob."	Empess du Marcoe
F. Simons.	"Bronco Jim."	Paul Neyron.
Mr. Crowell.	"Susie M."	Miss Garfield.
W. H. Syme.	"Claybank."	Gold of Ophir.
J. H. Outhwaite	"Euclid."	Papa Gontier.
C. A. Scharff.	"Faunie."	Metior.
A. B. Wilgus.	"Small Hopes"	Raymond Beauty.
Unknown.	"Daisy."	Cloth of Gold.
A. B. Anderson.	"Fire Fly."	Gen'l de Tartras.
A. B. Anderson.	"Gray Friar."	A. La Marc.
W. Volkmar.	"Great Hopes."	La France.
Arturo Bandini.	"Dimple."	Gloire Dijon.
W. Elliot.	"Rory O'Neil."	Banksia.

First Prize—Pair of Riding Boots, to be made to order by Wetherby & Kayser.
Second Prize—Lap Robe, valued at $25.
Third Prize—$10 Driving Whip.

15. Tug of War.

Pickwick vs. Duarte.

PICKWICK TEAM.

H. R. Hertel.	B. O. Kendall.
J. H. Cambell.	E. E. Fordham.
Edward E. Jones.	J. W. Lancaster.

16. Sack Race.

Ed. Buckius.   Dr. Harding.

Where Prizes are not mentioned they will be supplied.

Enterprising residents constantly sought new ways to entertain their annual visitors. They opened an exotic ostrich farm with boas and plumes for sale; they built an elevated cycleway for health-conscious cycling faddists; Professor Thaddeus Lowe constructed an incline railway to the top of a local mountain (now bearing his name), providing visitors with spectacular views all the way to the sea. The backyard of the Adolphus Busch home was terraced and landscaped. With the addition of a quaint mill, dwarf cottages, and terra-cotta fairy tale figures, Busch Gardens became the Disneyland of its day when it opened to the public in 1906.

Perhaps it was inevitable that this Western paradise would create a picture-postcard festival to publicize its attributes to the less fortunate East. London had her regal ceremonies, locals rea-

soned; Philadelphia her "Rose Tree Hunt;" Nice, France, her Battle of the Flowers. Pasadena would devise something to combine all three, and, according to Tournament founders, rival them in pomp, pageantry, and natural beauty. In 1889, Dr. Francis Rowland and Professor Charles Frederick Holder, with the help of their colleagues at the local Valley Hunt Club, came up with the notion of a Tournament of Roses. For those first few years, it would be nothing more than a modest procession of flower-covered carriages converging on a dusty park for a New Year's Day of picnicking and games, but it would grow to have a much wider significance.

"'Tournament of Roses'," the local newspaper declared, "is a name well adapted to convey to the blizzard-bound sons and daughters of the East, one of the sources of enjoyment which we, of the land of perennial sunshine boast." Here was an encapsulization of a dozen California dreams: home grown roses on the first of January, outdoor sports in the dead of winter, leisure and prosperity on parade, the superior beauty of California girls displayed, the prowess of her athletes proven. This was the perfect way to annually present the rest of America with Pasadena's latest installment of the California dream. And in ways the founders could never have guessed, it worked.

For example, in the early 1900s, in the afternoons after the Rose Parade, the Tournament put on chariot races inspired by Lew Wallace's novel *Ben Hur*. With hair-raising finishes and a few terrifying accidents (faithful to the novel), the races were big crowd-pleasers. They featured the pride of local stables, and of the citizens who mounted teams, no one was more colorful than Lucky Baldwin. "Lucky at the mines, lucky in the markets, lucky with horses, and luckiest of all with land," they used to say of Baldwin. Taking his immense profits out of the Comstock Lode, he bought part of the huge Rancho Santa Anita adjoining Pasadena in 1873. On it he built the gingerbread "Queen Anne's Cottage," familiar to TV viewers as the set for "Fantasy Island," and around it he planted trees, making it the future site of the Los Angeles Arboretum. In 1874, he bought a pair of Kentucky-bred stallions and started raising racehorses that would eventually bring in $100,000 a year in prize money. It is no surprise, then, that his chariot teams were among the most successful, a success that underscored his own fulfillment of a California dream. He epitomized the fortunes to be made in the West—in the mines, in real estate, and most elusive of all, through gambling. His legacy lives on today in the racetrack that was built on his former ranch—

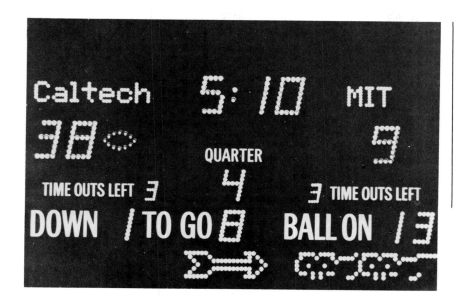

Caltech's triumphant return to mischief making in 1984 included hostage-taking of the scoreboard. The electronic sabotage declared the Techies sound winners over MIT.

Santa Anita, one of the country's finest venues for horse racing.

A generation later, the California dream that the Tournament publicized highlighted the Southland's rich cultural life. Hollywood starlets ornamenting floats told of the area's best-known contribution to pop culture. Cities like Los Angeles and Santa Barbara advertised their Spanish heritage and local fiestas. Laguna Beach entered a·float of the Last Supper to publicize its summer art festival where great paintings, like DaVinci's, were reproduced by costumed citizens. Nearby San Marino featured a float with Gainsborough's "Blue Boy" and Lawrence's "Pinkie" to remind viewers of its Huntington Library and Art Gallery, where the paintings could be seen.

Here at the Huntington was the good life in California as only the richest could afford it. Henry E. Huntington had transformed his dusty ranch into a felicitous combination of the Frick Collection, the Morgan Library, and a well-maintained Central Park. He could afford to spend lavishly, drawing on a $40 million inheritance from his uncle Collis P. Huntington, one of the builders of the Southern Pacific Railroad, or his own earnings as president of the Pacific Electric, L.A.'s first suburban railway. He would buy whole libraries—including a Gutenberg Bible, Benjamin Franklin's autobiography in his own hand, and the Ellesmere Chaucer. In his yard he planted rare palms, exotic fruit trees, succulents, and cacti, and for his home he collected fine French furniture, tapestries, and 18th-century English paintings.

When, in what virtually amounted to a corporate merger, he married his uncle's widow and other heir, Arabella Huntington, he wooed her with an authentic Japanese garden—presenting a landscape ideal that would profoundly influence Southern California gardening (and many a Rose Parade float). When he died in 1927, he left behind a dream that is today visited by thousands.

After World War II, the California dream became one of high technology. Business boomed in the defense and aerospace industries, with Pasadena's Jet Propulsion Laboratory and Caltech contributing scientific wizardry. Naturally, they became participants in the Tournament of Roses. JPL, world-famous for its Mariner and Voyager unmanned spacecraft missions, provided the theme for a number of space-oriented floats, and in 1963 even supplied a grand marshal: William Pickering, then company head. Caltech, with its countless Nobel laureates and dazzling discoveries in physics, medicine, chemistry, and aerodynamics, has made a more dubious contribution. Without a football team to compete in the Bowl, the school has made only unscheduled appearances in the annual game.

In 1961, a group of Techie student pranksters sabotaged the U. of Washington card section. At the half, 2,232 unknowing Husky fans created a splendid picture of the Caltech beaver. Then they spelled WASHINGTON backwards, and for their grand finale formed a glorious CALTECH. In 1981, the pranksters failed when they were apprehended at the Bowl trying to bury a hydraulically operated device that would release a helium-filled balloon labeled "Caltech" at halftime. But they made a triumphant return in 1984, taking over the scoreboard via radio control during the Illinois-UCLA game. In the third quarter it suddenly told the over 100,000 Bowl fans and millions of TV viewers: Caltech 38, MIT 9. Rumor has it the students were given classroom credit for their stunt. What better publicity for their alma mater's preeminence in electronics?

In recent years California has often dreamed about her own past. In the parade, there are countless recreations of long-gone eras—the romance of the missions or the pleasures of a lazy, turn-of-the-century picnic. Moreover, Pasadena, with more years behind her than most Southern California towns, has a rich supply of old homes to serve as a backdrop to the parade. A few, like the architecturally adventurous Gamble house, have been turned into museums. Several of the grandest mansions on South Orange Grove have been incorporated into Ambassador College. And one of the most elegant of all, the porticoed Wrigley Man-

sion, now serves as the permanent headquarters of the Tournament of Roses.

Grandiose indeed with its wide stairs, chandeliered halls, and paneled rooms, it is used today for receptions and meetings to plan the Rose Parade and Rose Bowl. Lights flood it before dawn on Parade day, and it becomes the setting for the television interviews that precede the parade broadcast. Evidently, the Wrigley can still pass as an example of gracious living. I recall a dinner my father hosted there during the year he was president of the Tournament. The honored guest was none other than Prince Philip, the Duke of Edinburgh. When dinner was over, the Duke turned to thank his hosts. Unaware that no one actually lives in the mansion, he said to my mother, "You have a lovely home." Mom just nodded and smiled.

But of all the dreams that intermingle in Pasadena, the one that first drew settlers to her continues to entrance visitors to the Tournament of Roses today. The avocado trees are heavy with fruit, the lawns are spring green with annual rye, the liquidambar trees look like New England maples in the fall, and the holly is studded with red berries. In January, it's as though all seasons were happening at once, with the heaviest emphasis on spring. The magnolias and pears are white with blossoms, the jacarandas are lavender, the camellia bushes are dotted with every color used on a Valentine. Beneath them the calla lilies open up and birds of paradise wave. And oh yes, roses, roses of every color, are in bloom in Pasadena on the first of January.

Opposite: Lucky Baldwin, sponsor of the triumphant 1909 chariot team, with his family on the grounds of his estate which today is the Los Angeles City Aboretum. Left: The William Wrigley Mansion, which was donated in 1960 to the city of Pasadena and the Tournament of Roses as headquarters.

2 · NEVER ON A SUNDAY

Once a year Pasadena goes a little mad. "No Parking" signs spring up on quiet residential streets that rarely see cars. Well-groomed front lawns resemble used car lots, with palms sporting placards, "Park and Walk to Parade. $15 All Day." A five-and-a-half-mile stretch of the city's usually orderly main streets, from South Orange Grove to Colorado then north on Sierra Madre, becomes what local policemen refer to as "the world's biggest New Year's Eve party." Spectators anxious to get the best spots for viewing the parade arrive on December 31, bringing sleeping bags, folding chairs, barbecues, and couches to spend the night in varying degrees of discomfort. Then at dawn, half the bleary-eyed all-nighters go home to recover from the excesses of their celebration, and miss the parade.

Buses, station wagons, RVs, motorcycles, pickups pulling horse trailers, and cyclists selling souvenirs pour into town; parade viewers pile on top of buildings, roofs, ladders, and chairs. They peer out of office windows and climb up trees like the biblical Lazarus—all to witness what has been called "the Hallelujah Chorus of Beauty" on the "Avenue of Awes." And then, as though that were not enough, over 100,000 football fans descend into the Arroyo Seco, emptying into America's most celebrated Bowl to see her oldest college Bowl game, the Granddaddy of Them All.

There are rules to this madness, certain inviolable customs and laws. First of all, the Pasadena Police Department has its regulations: no one can chain furniture to public property to reserve seats for the parade. The police will use boltcutters to remove items. No one can claim turf along the parade route until noon on December 31. (Some young entrepreneurs stay up all night, pacing to avoid Pasadena's loitering laws, and claim territory earlier than that, unlawfully renting it out to top bidders. A stretch wide enough for six chairs on Orange Grove recently went for $100.) And on New Year's Eve, there's no drinking allowed—although it seems that only the most flagrant abusers are arrested.

The sun rises at 6:57 a.m., hitting 5,710-foot Mount Wilson above town about a minute earlier. Starting time for the Parade varies—some years it's 8:00, other years it's 8:20 or 8:30—but it always starts exactly at the designated time. About a million people will see it in person—over 100,000 of them in grandstands. Another estimated 325 million from around the world will watch it on TV. It will last just over two hours, and when the tail leaves Orange Grove, the head will reach northern Sierra Madre, like a serpent stretching across town.

Preceding pages: Spectators jam every inch of viewing space along parade route. Opposite: Firestone's Atlantis entry and that year's theme, "Tales of the Seven Seas," were both apt presagers of the 1934 Tournament, one of the few times rain dampened the proceedings.

The game begins at 2:00 p.m. and must be over by 5:00, at which time the Orange Bowl is broadcast. The field will be in sunshine until halftime, when the long winter shadows require the Stadium's lights for the TV cameras. By the time they go out, 1,200 vendors at the Bowl will have sold 40,000 hot dogs, 900 kegs of beer, 40,000 sodas, 18,000 bags of peanuts, and 9,000 T-shirts. Also by day's end, three million pictures of the parade and game will have been taken, making the Tournament the single most photographed event in the world.

It will never rain on the Rose Parade and Rose Bowl. The last time it did was in 1955. And before that, it has only rained a half-dozen times, an amazing statistic considering the Tournament comes in the midst of California's rainy season. The sun and warmth will be a major attraction for TV viewers in the heart of Big Ten country, and beyond. According to the L.A. *Times*, on New

Above: It's never too early to stake out a front-row seat. Folding chairs, sleeping bags, and barbecues crop up the day before the parade. Opposite: Those who arrive during parade day will sit farther back—but with no less enthusiasm.

Year's morning in Fairbanks, Alaska, where outside it averages 34 degrees below zero, almost every TV is tuned to the parade.

No political controversy will spoil the event. The parade was only cancelled once, during World War II. Even then, a group of stalwarts from the Pasadena City College Lancer Band marched down Colorado Boulevard in the form of a "V" for "Victory," singing "Stout-Hearted Men." Earl Warren was picketed in the grandstands by civil rights demonstrators in 1965; Miss Watts on the L.A. float raised her clenched fist in the symbol of black power in 1971; the police thought they found a bomb on the Big Ten float in 1986 (it turned out to be part of the float's mechanism). But such events are anomalies. Dissension has no place here. Protestors, like the animal rights advocates who threatened one year to take all the flowers off a bullfighting float, are dismissed as spoilsports. After all, as 1987 grand marshal soccer star Pele noted, this is a parade of flowers—not missiles, tanks, and guns.

There will be around 60 floats, 25 equestrian units, and 22 marching bands, arranged so that humorous floats are mixed up with the simply beautiful ones, and bands from California are staggered among bands from around the world, and an Arabian horse unit does not follow another Arabian. Montie Montana will twirl his lariat, as he has in over 50 parades, and bystanders will say "Hi, George" to local talk-show host George Putnam on his palomino. The Salvation Army timbrelists will march in their black bonnets and black pumps, the Marines in their dress blues. After it's all over, everyone will exclaim, "It was the best Rose Parade ever!" And that night, the Pasadena Sanitation Department will collect 125 tons of trash, with an extra 20 soggy tons if it rains. (There were extra tons in 1982, when it poured cats and dogs *before* the parade. The sun burst through just as grand marshal Jimmy Stewart swung around the corner of Colorado and Orange Grove.)

The event goes like clockwork. A NASA rocket launch would not seem to require so much organization. The progress of the floats into the formation area is monitored from a trailer filled with Tournament volunteers talking urgently, munching doughnuts, downing coffee, and listening to one of 320 Tournament of Roses Radio Amateurs (TORRA) on his radio. A map shows the route the floats travel, to be filled in with red ink for each landmark passed. The bands and horses will feed in from side streets, weaving into a tight braid.

The volunteers wear red ribbons, just part of a bewildering array of badges, passes, and ribbons necessary to enter the formation area. Red are for officials, white for special guests, blue for guests of the Tournament of Roses president, light blue for float decorators, yellow for TV and radio staff, orange for media. The most coveted of all is the light orange ribbon labeled "Everywhere," a pass into the television staging areas, the Bowl press box, the float decorating places, and the bustling center of all this activity, Tournament headquarters in the former Wrigley Mansion.

The timetable is exact, dictating when the floats are to be ready for their final judging, when the bands must be tuned up and ready to go, when the equestrians need to mount their horses—after making one last stop at the portable restrooms that generously accommodate the area. Thick notebooks tell Tournament committee chairmen when barricades need to be manned, when streets are closed off to traffic, when parade participants must be on their floats, when breakfast is served, and when volunteers change out of their warm overalls into the white suits they have come to be identified with. Even President Reagan, who did the Rose Parade coverage on ABC and CBS for years, noted it. In 1986, at the signing of the bill that made the rose America's national flower, he pointed to his watch and said to the

Rose Queen, "You can set your watch by that parade." Down to the minute.

But once every seven years, this schedule goes awry—by 24 hours. On December 31, no one lines the streets. No one camps out that night with barbecues, beach chairs, TVs, chenille bedspreads, picnic stools, and card tables. No New Year's Eve games of chess, dominoes, Hearts, or Old Maid, no frisbees flying across the road, no midnight games of football. On New Year's Day the Rose Bowl is empty, except for a few groundskeepers working on the grass. Once every seven years, when New Year's lands on a Sunday, the Tournament of Roses is postponed for a day. The TV schedules are juggled, the float builders get an extra day to work on their creations, and the white suiters go to black-tie New Year's Eve parties for once in their lives. They will be back in white as the parade marches on Monday, January 2. But never, ever on a Sunday.

PROLOGUE

Even as the sanitation workers are collecting abandoned sofas, crates, and hibachis, the plans for the next Tournament are well underway. As early as December, 13 months in advance, the float builders get an indication of the theme for the subsequent parade. The themes are usually slogans: "On the Road to Happiness," "Through the Eyes of a Child," "The Good Life." Some sound like categories from charades—"Pages from the Ages," "Ballads in Blossoms," "Tall Tales and True." Others seem to repeat themselves: "Adventures in Flowers," "Adventures in Roses," "Around the World in Flowers."

However broad, the themes are meant to give the parade cohesion. In former days they were selected in a contest. The Tournament, deluged with postcards, awarded free parade and Bowl tickets (scarce as hen's teeth) to the winner for his ideas. These days, the theme is decided by the Tournament President. When my dad was president in 1983, he spent countless hours ruminating over the proper choice. He was considering "Faith and Family," then maybe "Free Enterprise," and at the time he spoke to the decorators, it was "Faith, Hope and Love." Then he changed his mind, and it became and remained "Rejoice!"—with an exclamation point at the end, the way he must have signed hundreds of Christmas cards.

The selection of the grand marshal also begins early, especially if the Tournament president is looking for a well-known

(and generally overbooked) celebrity. Everyone from the Pope to the Queen of England has been considered, although the final choice has often been a local hero. In 1979, the Tournament's own tireless volunteer Lay Leishman, former president and chairman emeritus of the football committee, was chosen. I remember Dad went through dozens of names before he settled on sportscaster, actor, former pro football player, and longtime Pasadena area resident (a neighbor of ours) Merlin Olsen. Dad did not even have to get in the car to ask Merlin. He and Mom walked down the street carrying a bouquet of roses.

The grand marshal usually has an obvious link to the theme—John Wayne and "Movie Memories"; Bonanza star Lorne Greene and "The Great Outdoors"; Lawrence Welk and "The Joy of Music." For James Boyle, Jr. when he was president, one of the floats suggested the perfect grand marshal. The theme that year was "Spirit of America" and Boyle knew the torch from the Statue of Liberty would be on the Hilton Hotels float. Why not the chairman of the Statue's restoration effort for the honor? Hence, Lee Iacocca led the parade in 1985.

Presidents get nervous if they do not have their man, or woman, in plenty of time. The 1974 president, Ted Wilson, jumped the gun a bit when he talked to cartoonist Charles Schulz a year and a half in advance. The creator of Snoopy, Charlie Brown, and Lucy was flattered and accepted. Then a month later, Schulz called Wilson in utter bewilderment. He had read in the papers that John Wayne was going to lead the upcoming parade. Wilson assured him that he simply had a year to go. When it was finally Schulz's turn, the Rose Parade turned up in his comic strip: Lucy is sitting in front of the TV. Linus walks up and asks, "What are you watching?" "The Rose Parade from Pasadena," Lucy replies. "Has the grand marshal gone by yet?" Linus inquires. "Yeah, you missed him," Lucy says, "but he wasn't anyone you ever heard of."

In the fall the grand marshal is announced in a ceremony for the media. Jimmy Stewart posed for pictures with his sidekick Harvey. Pele seemed amused to be carrying an American-style football. Humorist Erma Bombeck remarked about the Rose Bowl, "It's the first bowl I've ever seen that I didn't have to clean." After the announcement his year, Lee Iacocca was whisked upstairs at the Tournament House, where he posed for pictures with the Royal Court. It was Iacocca's only visit to Pasadena before the parade, and the Rose Queen had not been selected yet, so each princess tried on the crown and pretended she was queen.

Opposite: They come from near and very far. Although no tickets are needed for the parade, it helps to have them for the game, as the Rose Bowl is sold out well into the 21st century.

Above: Bands from across the country begin to move into position even before the sun comes up.
Opposite: The Tournament of Roses is a family affair.

TOURNAMENT TIME

By the fall, activities leading up to the Tournament begin in earnest. The queen is crowned in the Coronation at the Tournament House. She and her court make dozens of appearances around town, having their pictures snapped wherever they go. One queen remembers being photographed at the Los Angeles Arboretum in her white dress and crown. A tourist came up to her, wishing her well. "When's the big day?" the woman asked. "January 1," the queen replied, hiding her surprise at the woman's ignorance. "New Year's Day," the tourist said, shaking her head, "what an odd day to get married!"

The Pasadena Jaycees honor the queen and court at a brunch before Thanksgiving. The Tournament President is honored at a Pasadena Chamber of Commerce breakfast. Also in the fall, 1,750 people get the opportunity to buy 3,500 Rose Bowl tickets, the only tickets available to the general public (all the rest are distributed in the Pac-10/Big Ten, parade participants, and the Tournament membership). In an open lottery, their names are drawn out of a hat containing some 200,000 postcards—not very promising odds.

Signs of the coming pageant pop up about the time Christmas decorations appear. Tournament white suiters start driving around town in the white "official Tournament of Roses cars," 90 Oldsmobiles bearing temporary "T of R" license plates. You can tell which one belongs to the President: his plate bears the number One. Grandstands rise on lawns, parking lots, Christmas tree lots—on any square foot of space along Orange Grove, Colorado, and Sierra Madre Boulevards. They wrap around department ment stores, gas stations, churches, and schools, making up what is said to be the largest temporary-seating installation in the world. The only holdout seems to be the Norton Simon Museum, whose bronze Rodins and Lachaises remain oblivious to the celebration outside their garden walls.

Perhaps the surest sign of the parade's arrival is the repainting of the blue and rose lines. The rose line marks the center of the parade route, so that float drivers and marching bands can follow it down the boulevard. The blue "honor line," painted seven feet from the curb, defines the parade seating area. Viewers are not allowed to venture beyond it, nor can they move up to it until midnight on New Year's Eve—creating a stampede that has often been compared to the Oklahoma Land Rush. The idea for the blue lines was inspired by the honor lines at community

41

Above and opposite top: Box seats and front-row mezzanine are provided by both the office buildings of Pasadena and personal RVs. **Opposite bottom:** Although possibly not needed, mounted police help maintain the smooth flow of floats.

dances in the '30s. There, women stood behind one line and men behind another, only crossing it to dance; as Lay Leishman said, "Can you imagine this happening today?"

Meanwhile, across the country, high school bands are raising their last thousand dollars, holding one more pancake breakfast, having one more car wash, so they can pay for the trip to California. Flower growers in Colorado and Hawaii are monitoring their crops destined for the parade. In the Midwest and the West, the selection of the best football teams from the Big Ten and Pac-10 is narrowing. At the game where the winner of each conference is determined, the President of the Tournament is on hand to award the victors roses and their well-deserved invitation to the Bowl. In November 1985, when it looked like Arizona State was going to the Bowl for the first time, James Boyle, Jr. was on the sidelines with roses at the end of the game. But then, as fate would have it, ASU's archrival Arizona made a last-second fieldgoal, winning the game, sending the Rose Bowl bid back to UCLA. Boyle quickly dashed the roses under a tarp, not without being noticed by a sports photographer. "Get out of here," Boyle snarled in mock anger.

Back in Pasadena, the city turns out for an unofficial—and not always appreciated—pre-parade parade, a parody of the Tournament of Roses. Conceived in a local beer bar, the "Occasional" Doo Dah Parade was inaugurated on New Year's Day 1978, when New Year's was on a Sunday. Every year since, it has meandered through Old Pasadena on the Sunday after Thanksgiving, attracting a crowd of 50,000 with its motley marchers. There are the mutant queens who do a nuclear energy spoof and whose members include Olivia Neutron Bomb and Agnes Warhead. There are motorless floats, papier mache horses, belly dancers, tap dancers, marching kazoo players, and the all-time favorite, the Synchronized Briefcase Drillteam, who insist they rehearse no more than 45 minutes a year (to see them is to believe it). Although it is not always greeted with enthusiasm, the Doo Dah is an institution (how they would shudder to hear the word) flattering by imitation its none-too-amused parent.

KICKOFF

Before Christmas, the first guests to arrive in Southern California for the Tournament are the football teams. For many years the Big Ten teams stayed at the Huntington Sheraton, one of Pasadena's dowager resort hotels. These days, visiting teams stay

maned Senator Everett Dirksen was grand marshal in 1968, he attended the Palladium dinner, and on his way in, according to former Pasadena *Star News* sports editor Joe Hendrickson, he stopped at the lady at the ticket window. "Now put your mouth up to the round hole, and give me a kiss," he said. He got one, too.

In Pasadena, on December 30, a half-dozen of the bands marching in the parade perform sample halftime shows on the Pasadena City College football field. Band Fest, it's called. Although not a competition, it's a good opportunity for the bands to compare routines which they cannot normally show off in the parade. Twirlers twirl, drum majors strut, flag bearers march in complicated formations, and instrumentalists step forward for solos. Among the crowds in the PCC stands are hundreds from the Good Sam Club, an organization of RV owners.

Every year the Good Sams camp out on the City College grounds for their annual Rose Parade Samboree. The Band Fest and parade are only half the fun. For a busy week the mostly retired Good Sambassadors (as they are called) can attend seminars on subjects such as Social Security, fishing, refrigeration and propane gas; they can learn exercises to do "in their rigs"; they go square dancing or play "Samgo," the Good Sam's version of Bingo. They tour the floats being decorated, trade traveling tips, bring in the New Year with Lawrence Welk star Jo Ann Castle, watch the parade, watch the game on TV, and after it's all over, they only have to go as far as their rigs to be home.

Out in front of the PCC Samboree campground, on Colorado Boulevard, the last few obstructions are coming down—the stoplights, telephone lines, and street lights that are too low for the floats. At the Bowl, the turf has just been painted, covered with nearly 1,200 gallons of Environcolor, a water-soluble vinyl acetate with special additives to keep the grass healthy. The design for the colored end zones, bearing the names of the teams, is drawn by local architect Don Murphy, approved by the two football conferences, and executed by the Pasadena Jaycees. Every colored area needs two coats of paint, and at night tarps to protect them from the dew. In the rare instance of rain, huge fans and even a helicopter have been used to dry the field.

The Kiwanis Kickoff Luncheon takes place a day or two before New Year's. Held in the Pasadena Convention Center, it has the distinction of being the largest service club luncheon in the world. Not only is the US Kiwanis leadership in attendance, but national and international presidents from other service clubs

are as well: the National Exchange Club, Rotary, the American Legion, the Jaycees. They and some 4,000 other guests meet the football coaches and teams, and feast on a box lunch that has always been the object of good-natured ridicule: chicken salad sandwich on a dry roll, watery coleslaw, raisins masquerading as grapes. At the 1980 lunch, when grand marshal Lorne Greene opened up his box, he discovered a can of dog food. The Kiwanians looked at it with mock surprise, and promptly brought him a new box with the customary "Feast."

For years Pasadenan Bill Symes has been the luncheon emcee. His voice is familiar to football fans because he also makes the public announcements at the Bowl. Back in 1940, Symes played for Stanford in the Bowl, playing for only the last minute. Having been one of the substitutes, he's especially careful to learn

Opposite: 1985's Grand Marshal, Lee Iacocca, poses with Kristina Smith, who would later be named Rose Queen.
Above left: The Doo Dah Parade, conceived in 1978 as a parody of the real thing, meanders through Pasadena the Sunday after Thanksgiving, and features a mutant queen.
Above right: Innovative seating.

all the names on both teams. "If some poor guy gets in the game at the last minute," he says, "I want to give him credit." At the Kickoff Luncheon, he shares the dais with the NBC game announcers, Dick Enberg and Merlin Olsen, and they interview players. For all the polite repartee between coaches, captains, and teams, it's clear that the tension is mounting. There will not be much time for repartee later.

TELEVISION

For many years the Kickoff Luncheon was broadcast locally over KTTV, with commentary by the redoubtable Bill Welsh. Welsh has been announcing the parade ever since 1948, the second year it was televised. He could not have known then what an enormous influence the medium would have on the Tournament. Today, just in Pasadena, the parade is broadcast over eight different TV stations, two of them Spanish-speaking. NBC, CBS, Fox, Tribune, Spanish International, and Telmundo carry it across the country. In Los Angeles, KTTV and KTLA broadcast it several times during the day—so that when you go home after the Bowl, you can watch the parade once again, looking for all that you missed because of a hangover or the large lady obstructing your view. On some stations there are no commercial interruptions. The networks, on the other hand, often use it as an opportunity to plug new shows. One year Nabisco bought advertising on both networks to introduce a new, three-note jingle.

Recently, the Tournament has pushed to increase its international exposure. Videospec International broadcasts the parade via satellite to an astonishing number of countries: France, Taiwan, Argentina, Japan, Italy, Malaysia, Mexico, Hong Kong, Singapore, and Australia. On January 1 (or the day after, as the broadcast crosses the dateline), the parade reaches a foreign audience of hundreds of millions. As Lay Leishman often says of the Tournament, "like Topsy, it just growed." The only place it's difficult to market the parade is in the Mideast—"because of cheerleaders with pompoms and short skirts and girls twirling batons," says Videospec's Dick Auerbach. "It's difficult to take anything there where women are not dressed in the manner they think proper."

Because of this phenomenal exposure, companies are willing to spend thousands of dollars on floats, and marching bands from across the country clamor to be seen on TV. Working with the pressure of all those TV schedules, the Tournament knows it

must keep the parade moving, getting it past the cameras in the requisite two hours. For every band cut or float missed because the parade ran too long, they will receive hundreds of angry letters and phone calls, each deserving an explanation and apology. The Tournament refuses to pander to cameras' excessive demands—they will not allow celebrities on floats to be interviewed during the parade. Cameramen are not permitted to take portable cameras out in the street in the line of march, spoiling another station's shot. Floats must be designed to appear from all angles, not just the camera-popular right side. But even so, everyone knows the parade is not simply for the million who see it in person.

The filming of the parade presents its own challenges. One of the biggest is to capture all of a continuously moving event, while still breaking for commercials (at least in the Rose Bowl, there are conveniently called time-outs). What NBC does, for example, is to film *up* the parade route, spending about a minute and 15 seconds on each unit until a commercial. Then they leave the parade "upstream." When they come back after a break, they catch whatever they have missed "downstream" on Colorado and slowly move back up to the corner of Orange Grove . . . until the next break.

In the Bowl and during the parade, the Tournament makes a special effort to maintain quality. If you have ever wondered why you do not see the usual "Hi, Mom," "Send Money," or "Jesus Saves" signs at the Rose Bowl (except in the UCLA card section), it's because the stadium is strictly policed. As soon as the signs go up, an official pulls them down. There are no fights in the stands shown, no couples necking, no cameras lingering over scantily clad fans. NBC, with its 12 cameras, is asked to concentrate on the football teams, the bands, and the cheerleaders. As director Harry Coyle says, "You give us a presentation with dignity and we'll televise it with dignity."

NEVER ON A SUNDAY

Dignity and durability, perhaps that's what brings fans back to Pasasdena—like swallows returning to Capistrano. They know what to expect on January 1: fun, color, excitement, as well as waiting in line, straining your neck, and fighting the traffic in what Bob Hope once called "The Tournament of Fenders." The event will come off exactly as it has in years past . . . except it's always better every year.

Colorado Boulevard, the main thoroughfare for the parade. Spectators are seated early, as the parade begins at 8:30 in the morning and is all finished two hours later.

There will be celebrities on the floats, as in years past: Sonny and Cher (when they were together), Tommy LaSorda (after winning and losing seasons), Lawrence Welk (a perennial favorite), Anne Murray, Dinah Shore (whose gold lame dress was once singed by a heater on her float), Tracy Austin, Hilo Hattie, Rod McKuen, even Rin Tin Tin. There will be distinguished guests in the stands, people like Earl Warren, who once estimated that he had seen the Tournament 35 times. He kept coming long after he had left California politics for his seat on the Supreme Court bench. Like him, comedian Harold Lloyd was a regular on the sidelines, taking pictures. Richard and Pat Nixon came to the parade and game on their first date in 1939, and returned often.

There will be vendors hawking hats, T-shirts, frisbees, yoyos, film, pompoms, pennants, and in the cloudless sky, skywriters advertising beer, amusement parks, and real estate developments. There have been kooks who wanted to get married in the Rose Bowl—with the captains of the two teams as groomsmen and the Rose Court as bridesmaids. Once a Bowl player got married on the first (USC's guard Elmer Willhoite in 1953) although not in the Bowl, and a pair of float drivers were once married New Year's Eve—in 1982, atop the City of Montebello's float with the Flintstone cartoon characters in attendance.

Fans will yell "play, play" as the bands pass, and the Marines will oblige with "From the Halls of Montezuma" and the Salvation Army with "Onward Christian Soldiers." The Pac-10 band or Big Ten band will launch into a fight song sure to bring half a stand to its feet (the other half will merely clap courteously). Youngsters will run out into the street when floats drop flowers, picking up a mum or carnation for their mothers. The queen and princesses will forget their decorum and start waving with both hands. Bathing beauties on floats will fight off the early morning cold with toothy grins, responding to requests for their phone numbers with broader grins. Around the Bowl, tailgaters will set up elaborate picnics, and after the game many of them will forget where they left their RVs and cars.

The floats will be on view for several days after the parade, and after that scavengers will seek to collect their blossoms for hospital bouquets or potpourri or rosary beads. Other than that, there's not much left when it's all over—snapshots, pins, programs, perhaps a newspaper clipping or two. At least there's the assurance that it will happen again next year. And the next. And the next.

But never, ever on a Sunday.

The Tournament of Roses presents its own special challenges to photographers and television crews alike. The parade is televised by eight different TV stations and is received over satellite by countries worldwide.

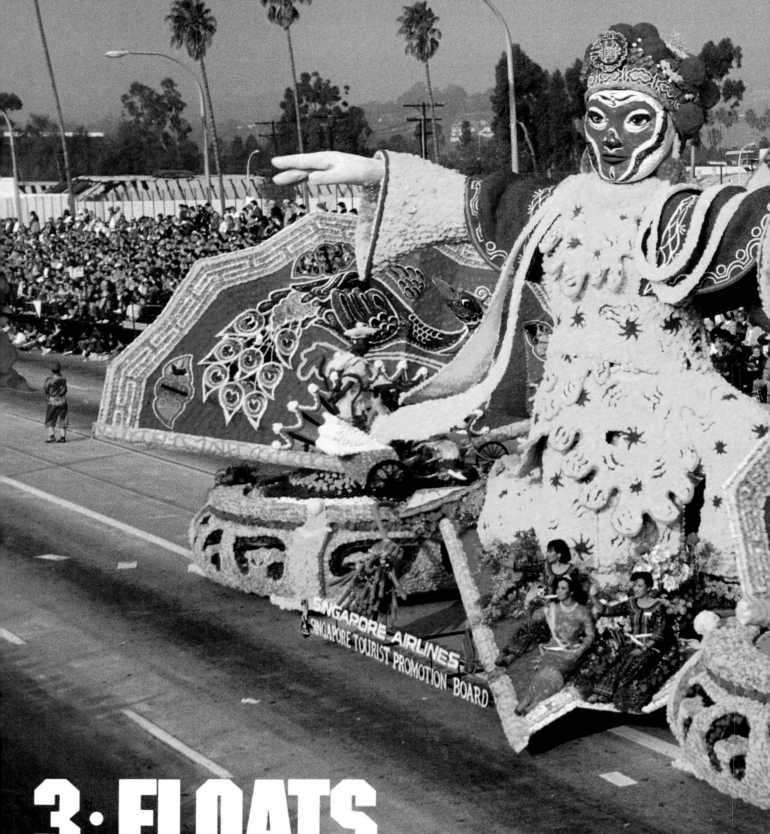

3· FLOATS
AND FLOWERS

SINGAPORE CELEBRATES
The Legend of the
Monkey God Festival

It's eleven o'clock on New Year's Eve, several miles from the parade route with its all-night party, cruising cars, and chaperoning white suiters. Here on a normally sleepy suburban boulevard in South Pasadena, lined with royal palms and crepe myrtle, a different crowd assembles. Groups of formally dressed dinner partiers linger at the curb, the women clutching their shawls in the cool night air, the men holding drinks. Children in their pajamas sit in cars with their parents at the side of the road. They are watching, peering into the fog, looking for the red and blue flash of police cars escorting a convoy of surrealistic shapes.

Suddenly they appear: floral wings of a bird in flight, a ship set to sail, a reclining Aztec warrior. A giant fountain trembles as it goes over a dip in the road, shaking thousands of iris, lilies, and orchids. A dragon rises out of the dark, his seaweed eyes glistening, his pink poinsettia gums moist, his white lunaria teeth catching the streetlamps' glow. The procession of trees, animals, a sphinx, a pagoda, makes its way through the night, heading towards the parade route, shepherded by a dozen white suiters and some of the floats' builders. "Will the ship make it under that stoplight?" they worry. "Did the fountain hit the tree at that corner? Did the dragon lose any roses coming around the bend?"

Each float will make its premiere appearance in less than ten hours. Each float will vie for a prize. Each represents the culmination of over a year's work for the builder, a year and a half of planning for the sponsor, months of tireless community fundraising, months of cultivation for the flower growers,and too many sleepless nights for the kids who decorated it. And in a few days, when the tulips have lost their petals and the roses are limp, the floats will be towed back to their builders to be disassembled, the steel scrapped, the hydraulic parts saved, the chassis and engines reused, so the process can begin once again for the next Rose Parade.

THE SPONSOR

The process starts with the sponsor. A full year and a half before the parade, the Tournament begins looking at entries. There's room for just 60 floats and the Float Entries Committee tries to keep a balance of commercial entries—Fortune 500 companies, banks, airlines, tourist boards—and non-commercial entries such as cities, universities, and service clubs. Longtime parade participants are invariably invited back—unless they have

Clockwise from upper left: Giorgio of Beverly Hills' 1987 entry, "A World of Elegance," recreated the Neptune fountain at Versailles; float designer Raul Rodriguez; in 1987 Farmer's Insurance celebrated statehood with the Mississippi River's "Delta Queen"; the Baskin-Robbins pastel-colored 1986 Happy Birthday float; Honda's immensely popular and intricate float of King Kong.

somehow offended the Tournament. Richard Frank, whose family started Lawry's Prime Rib restaurants, tells of the successful floats the family business had in the parade in the '30s, when the Tournament could ill-afford to be choosy about whom they let in. After a Lawry's float won the Sweepstakes in 1939, Richard's father decided Lawry's could take a year off. A Pasadena resident, he assumed that his chums in the Tournament would understand. On the contrary, his friends refused to let him back in the parade the next year, or the year after that or the year after that; Pasadenans have long memories. It was not until the early '70s that Lawry's Foods, Inc. (now a division of Lipton Tea) returned to the parade, and then it was only after Richard was coaxed into applying.

It's such stories that make float entrants cling to a berth in the Rose Parade as though it were a season ticket to the Giants' games or a box seat at the Hollywood Bowl. Nevertheless, over a half-dozen slots open up every year. To find the right newcomers, the Tournament sends form letters to over a hundred possible participants, then chooses 30 or 40 serious contenders. These they court for several months, "massaging them," as one Tournament committeeman describes it.

They go over the rules, explaining that every float must be completely covered with "fresh foliage, and other vegetation either dried or fresh." They give the prospective sponsor an idea of the costs—anywhere from $50,000 to over $200,000. They warn him that it's not an opportunity to advertise a new product or publicize a new service. "Thou shalt not sell soap in the Rose Parade," as one builder puts it. Instead, the Tournament lures prospective sponsors with its extraordinary public relations benefits. A float is an opportunity for a company, a city, or organization to get its name in the public eye. Each float is known by its sponsor's identity; the name is broadcast over the air and identified by a discreet sign on the float. With a national TV audience of well over 125 million (and perhaps as many as 325 million viewers worldwide), the parade is a real bargain. The Tournament estimates the sponsors' costs to be a phenomenally low one six-thousandth of a cent ($.0000016) per contact made.

The Tournament often makes an effort to include sponsors who are celebrating major anniversaries, such as United Way on its centennial or Pepperdine University on its 50th. Sometimes a particular parade theme will bring in certain sponsors. In 1987, with the theme "A World of Wonders," the Tournament attracted new entries from internationally-based firms like the Tourist De-

velopment Corporation of Malaysia and China Airlines. They try to make room for old standbys; nearby cities Sierra Madre, South Pasadena, and Burbank have had self-built, self-decorated floats in the parade since early in the century. And they seem to be impartial when it comes to service clubs and fraternal organizations: they include both Kiwanis and Rotary, the Elks and the Masons. They are even unbiased towards other pageants. The Portland Rose Festival has sponsored a float in the parade since 1912.

THE RIGHT IDEA

Once a sponsor has been accepted, it works with a professional builder (at last count there were ten in the Pasadena area) to find the right idea for its float. For Giorgio of Beverly Hills, the perfumer and retailer, in its first parade appearance in 1987, that idea was elegance. A recreation of the Neptune fountain at Versailles, the float featured a statue of the Roman god covered in silverleaf, riding a chariot pulled by dolphins of eucalyptus leaf amidst splashing "water" of iris and lilies. Arrayed around the fountain were a dozen models wearing designer dresses to convey "A World of Elegance," the float's title. The float did not need to spray Giorgio perfume in its wake to make its point. (Besides, the use of any perfume on a float, other than the natural aroma of the flowers, is against Tournament rules.) It said "elegance" well enough to win a prize for its builder, Fiesta Floats, and its sponsor.

Singapore Airlines, in cooperation with the Singapore Tourist Promotion Board, has been a very popular entrant in the parade for several years. In 1986, their theme was "Singapore Celebrates the Legend of the Monkey God Festival." C. E. Bent & Son built them a float showing a giant masked figure in a Chinese opera costume. The figure directed the mischievous antics of seed-covered minions of the Monkey God. Alongside it were stiltwalkers and acrobats doing flips and jumps and handstands on the unforgiving asphalt of Colorado Boulevard. The float was a rousing success, both in publicizing the allure of Singapore and winning the Sweepstakes Trophy, the parade's highest float honor.

In recent years, Farmers Insurance has chosen to honor a different state of the Union (one with many good customers) in the parade. In 1986, it was Texas on her sesquicentennial; another year it was Missouri, featuring a floral reconstruction of the Mississippi River showboat the "Delta Queen." Farmers Insurance always arranges to have the governor of the state riding on the float to give it added recognition. In fact, when Oklahoma governor George Nigh was riding in a replica of the fringe-topped surrey from the film "Oklahoma" on a float called "Rejoice in Oklahoma," a man stepped from the sidelines, yelling, "Hey, Governor, remember me?" Nigh smiled and waved, assuming it was one of his law-abiding constituents. Then the man identified himself: "You signed my pardon!"

Sometimes the connection between what a float says and what the sponsor does can be a subtle point of publicity. Baskin-Robbins Ice Cream Co. usually has playful floats: a carousel horse, a teddy bear popping out of a cake, a friendly Loch Ness Monster winding its way down the parade route. Only the colors, a pinkish palette of gladiolas, carnations, camellias, and roses, say Baskin-Robbins. One year their entry was made up of 31 characters, individually powered units, but did anyone notice that they

Opposite: In 1982 Avon won the Grand Prize for their stunning creation "Beauty of the Orient" to honor the company's Japanese affiliates. Unfortunately, the geisha girl depicted at the front of the float turned out not to be a geisha at all. Below: The City of Alhambra's 1973 entry, "Adventures of Tom Sawyer."

corresponded in number to the company's fabled 31 flavors of ice cream? Long Beach, one of Southern California's major port cities, often has an aquatic theme for its floats, so it was no surprise that its '86 float featured a goose water-skiing over a sea of statice and ornamental kale. But half the fun was realizing that this "spruce" goose—dressed in a tuxedo, top hat, and spats—correlated to the Long Beach tourist attraction, Howard Hughes's pioneer jumbo airplane, the Spruce Goose.

Occasionally a company's attempts at garnering specific publicity can backfire. In 1982 Avon Products wanted to honor its Japanese affiliates and so they produced a float with a Far Eastern theme, "Beauty of the Orient." At its front was a 15-foot geisha girl in a beautiful floral kimono. The float was a big high in the parade and won the Grand Prize. Avon sent pictures of the prize-winner to its Japanese subsidiaries, assuming they would be run in the local press. Nothing happened. After much prodding, the very polite Japanese businessmen explained that something was terribly wrong. "It turned out the woman we had portrayed wasn't a geisha at all," says Bill Corbett, former head of public relations for Avon. "She was something called an 'arrang,' which is like a lady of the night, or a very high-priced call girl. She had a long, flowing gown that could be pushed aside for . . . for obvious reasons. The Japanese were very embarrassed, but they wouldn't say anything beforehand. They wouldn't say, 'Hey, you've got it wrong.'" In a subsequent float honoring Thailand, Bill was very careful to have the design approved first by Avon's Thai staffers.

Even overwhelming success can have its drawbacks. Take the example of Honda's '87 crowd-pleaser, "King Kong—The Eighth Wonder of the World." One of the highly animated "blockbuster" floats built by Festival Artists for Honda, it featured a giant gorilla, crafted of black seaweed and coco palm fiber. The ape rose from a crouched position to an impressive 34-foot height, carrying a trembling blonde (the TV actress Cezanne Trimble) in his hand. He moved his head as he hungrily eyed her, pounded his chest in lust, and then brought her to his pink mouth, colored with crushed strawberries. The float won the award for animation and was clearly one of the most popular items in the parade. The sponsor, American Honda, was pleased. "It was our Christmas card to the world," Willie Tokishi, Honda's V.P. of Community Relations, says in describing his company's philosophy behind the float. But Rick Chapman, the builder, was not entirely satisfied.

Of course, he was justifiably proud of the technical achievement that made Kong possible and he was grateful for the

Opposite: In 1988 Casablanca Fan presented their "The World Is Not Flat." The float, deemed too large for judging, was entered in the "extra-ordinary" category.
Below: Not everything on a float is a flower.

gorilla's popularity, but he was hesitant because Kong and his Fay Wray look-alike upstaged their sponsor. "As it worked out," Chapman says, "Honda got their mentions, but King Kong and Cezanne Trimble were the stars of the Rose Parade . . . My goal is to get everybody to say, 'Did you see the Honda float? It was great!' not, 'Did you see the King Kong float?'"

A LITTLE PUBLICITY

Don Anderson, formerly of Fiesta Floats, put it more bluntly when he said, "We are not precisely in the business of making floats covered with flowers. We are working in the business of helping people get publicity." That means not just building the float but getting it seen, and not just on the parade route. Builders will work with their clients to sponsor pre-parade press conferences at the building sites. Sponsors will send out press releases announcing the personalities riding on the float, or pictures of the design and photos showing it being decorated. In 1982, when Anderson was building a float titled "Elks Serve Children Everywhere" for the Elks, he helped organize a ceremony dedicating it to the children of strife-torn Poland. The dedication, featuring Polish-American youngsters dressed in costume, received huge media coverage because of the timely nature of the subject. In 1987, Cal Poly Universities of Pomona and San Luis Obispo's float "Breaking the Ice," which showed penguins frolicking around a submarine, was christened at its decorating site by the captain of the Navy's nuclear submarine USS Pasadena, an event duly noted (and protested by some) in the press.

"If you've done your job right as a publicity person," Bill Corbett says, "you've got your money's worth out of the parade long before it even takes off on parade day." Of course, the 30 seconds that the float spends in front of the TV camera are crucial, but sponsors also try to get their float riders interviewed on camera before the parade (no one on a float is allowed to be interviewed *during* the parade) and to have the float decoration filmed for pre-parade broadcast. In 1987, Corbett, working for the American Institute of CPAs, was even able to get a video insert of his organization's president wishing America "Happy New Year" on the NBC broadcast as the AICPA float went by.

Internal publicity, too, can be just as important as external exposure for some sponsors. The float can be a means for generating internal or community morale. It will be written about in the company "rag" or the community newspaper, with a trivia quiz

Above: Isabella Coleman, "the Queen of Float Builders." She started constructing floats in 1904, won hundreds of awards, and was responsible for many advances and innovations. Opposite: A modest "float" from the year 1905.

on the Rose Parade—first prize a free trip to Pasadena for New Year's Day. Or there will be a contest to pick several citizens or employees to ride on the float. "It's the company picnic," says Rick Chapman, speaking both literally and figuratively.

On December 28, 29, and 30, there will be sponsor parties at the decorating site, serving everything from hamburgers and hot dogs to champagne and caviar. During a three-day period in 1987, over 3,000 Carnation Company employees and clients visited Festival Artists to see Carnation's "A Garden Full of Wonder." Some glued on a petal or two, but most just took in the spectacular sight: the rose petals outlined in black onion seeds to create giant butterfly wings, the enormous thistles made out of exotic pincushion protea blossoms, the brilliant yellow dendrobium orchids forming huge feathery flowers. It won the Sweepstakes Trophy that year, and all of Carnation watching the parade could say, "That's our float. *We* won!"

THE BUILDERS

It was not Rick Chapman's first butterfly-covered Sweepstakes winner. Eighteen years earlier, when Rick was in his twenties, he built a float of monarch butterflies returning to Monterey for the city of Los Angeles. Back then, he was just starting out, working in a flower shop and doing floats on the side. Los Angeles was one of only two clients, and he had no artist to paint a rendering of their float. Nor, as he says, did he have a talent for drawing. Four days before he was scheduled to make his presentation to the City Council, he decided he'd better improvise.

"I bought some paint and some brushes," he recalls, "got in my car and went down to Mexico and stayed on the beach for four days, believing that artists have magic brushes. I didn't realize that researching wouldn't hurt . . . I drew for two days from memory until I got something that I thought looked like a monarch butterfly. Then I painted for two days—I must have put 20 pounds of paint on it." The paint-encrusted rendering was approved by the City Council and the prize-winner, "Springtime Fantasy," established Rick's reputation as a builder. But since then, Rick has never done his own drawings for his firm, Festival Artists; as he says, "I figured I'd stop while I was ahead."

Like Rick, many people who make the floats seem to have entered the trade by chance. Take the example of Lotsie Busch Giersch, the "producer" (as she calls herself) of the St. Louis float. In 1955, she had recently moved to Pasadena from her native St.

Floats
of
Yesteryear

1908

1894

1895

1910

1904

1904 **Throop Polytechnic Institute (now Caltech)**

1918 **Los Angeles College**

Floats of Yesteryear
(continued)

1928 Moose Lodges—"The Heart of the World."

1925 Notre Dame's entry.

1936 Southern Pasadena Sweepstakes winner

1939 Floragraph of "The Last Supper."

1921 Elks lodge, still standing.

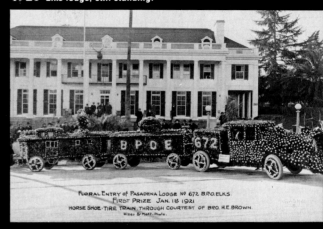

FLORAL ENTRY OF PASADENA LODGE Nº 672 B.P.O. ELKS.
FIRST PRIZE JAN. 1ST 1921
HORSE SHOE-TIRE TRAIN, THROUGH COURTESY OF BRO. H.E. BROWN.

1938 Long Beach's "Queen of Fantasy,"

1928 Beverly Hills' "Kingdom of Paradise."

Louis and attended the parade. Because she was the great-granddaughter of Aldophus Busch, founder of Anheuser-Busch brewery, and since her family's company had underwritten the St. Louis entry, she had more than just a passing interest in it. But when she saw the St. Louis float, a castle pulled by the Anheuser-Busch team of stocky Clydesdales, she was appalled. "Horses don't pull castles," she complained. She spoke to her father, then president of the company, and volunteered to supervise the design and production of the next float. And ever since then, under Lotsie's supervision, the Clydesdales have pulled wagons, carts, a stagecoach, a calliope, the English Coronation carriage—anything but a castle.

On the other hand, some *know* they are meant to build floats, and they know at a very young age. Raul Rodriguez was only 14 years old when he entered Whittier's contest to design the city's float for the Rose Parade. The theme that year was "Tall Tales and True," so Raul went to the library and looked for poems by the city's namesake, John Greenleaf Whittier. There he found the poem "Snowbound" and it became his title for a "snow"-covered float—icicles in trees, the north wind blowing, and girls in red capes. His design won the contest, the float was in the 1961 parade, and Raul has been designing imaginative floats ever since. These days he rides on one of his floats in the parade with a pet macaw on his shoulder.

A float builder is part floral designer, part publicist, part salesman and part mechanic. (Don Bent of C. E. Bent & Son originally started out in the auto-repair business.) It's a profession with nerve-wracking imponderables: shifting tastes, clients who change their minds, freezes that affect the flower crop, last-minute glitches in a float's animation, engine breakdowns. Some years a slow parade can prevent a float from passing in front of the TV cameras in time to be on the air—to a sponsor's great dismay. (As the builders reiterate, "99.9 percent of a sponsor's budget is spent for the camera.") It's not a lucrative business, most builders admit. "The floats are all prototypes," Don Bent declares. "They're underpriced. If it wasn't for our egos, the clients wouldn't be getting what they get." Bent himself has said he doesn't make his money on the Rose Parade. He makes it by reusing props from his floats in other parades. Even so, what makes float building appealing is the same thing that lures a painter to starve in a garret apartment or a musician to live on tuna and crackers. It's an art . . . with a healthy dose of carnival hucksterism thrown in.

The original artist in the Rose Parade, the person to whom

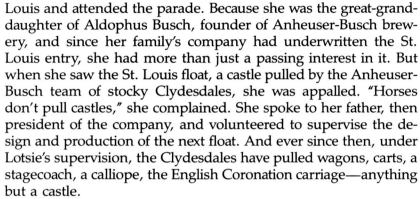

Below: The City of Barstow's 1950 entry, "Home On The Range."
Opposite: In 1967, Calgary, future home to the winter Olympics, offered their celebration of Canada's one-hundredth birthday.

CITY OF BARSTOW

HOME ON THE RANGE

the art of the floral float owes the most, was Isabella Coleman. She decorated her horse and buggy in 1910 and won second prize in her division. By 1913, she had her own float-decorating business and won first prize for her first client, the Pasadena realty board. For the next 59 years she built exotic peacocks, firebirds, dragons, and swans, earning prize after prize. A painstaking perfectionist, she was always looking for ways to make her floats better and introduced many of the innovations that led to the evolution of the modern float.

She was the first to weave flowers in and out of a chicken wire frame rather than tie them onto the float's structure. She was the first to use glue, pasting the flowers onto the float's body to give it a uniform texture and color. She introduced the use of test tubes to hold the more delicate roses and orchids in water. (Now the builders use plastic vials specially made for the purpose.) She was probably the first to use styrofoam figures. She was one of the first to use polyvinyl sprayed over chicken-wire frames—"cocooning," it's called; it was once used to mothball World War II ships. She was the first to build float chassis with airplane wheels to bring them down low, so they would pass viewers like a Persian carpet, only a few feet above the ground. She was also the first to keep the driver concealed, to maneuver his craft hidden beneath the chicken-wire frame.

With her fanatical attention to detail, Mrs. Coleman could be a taxing employer. Only days before the parade she would ask her workers to tear down a float and start over again—all because a canopy hung too low, or the plumage of a bird's feather had acquired an odd angle. Expense was no object. She ran her business as though it were a hobby, exasperating the IRS. She always kept her personal and business funds in the same bank account; if at the end of the year she had more money in it, she figured she'd made some money on her floats; if she had less, she figured she'd lost some. A dyed-in-the-wool Republican, she once saw a car parked in the Coleman lot bearing a Kennedy sticker and threatened to fire whoever owned it. Fortunately for the employee, she never found out.

BUILDING A FLOAT

The steps for building a float have not changed much since Isabella Coleman's day. A specially built chassis with a heavy motor and an extra large radiator is covered with a wood or metal frame. It is then wrapped in screening (window screening is more

Preceding pages: Closeup of figure from China Airlines' "So Far and Yet So Near." Right: The Marine Corps band precedes floats from Giorgio Beverly Hills and First Interstate Bank. Opposite: "Bully For the British," presented by the city of Torrance, California.

often used these days than chicken wire) and sprayed with a polyvinyl cocooning. The cocooning is painted with the colors of the flowers to go on it and the floats are then decorated. What *has* changed since Mrs. Coleman was in business are the number of variations on this system, and the timetable the builders must follow.

In February, almost a year before the parade, the builders assemble at the Tournament House to submit their ideas in rounds to the Float Entries Committee. For each float in the parade, the builders (and the half-dozen self-built entrants) are allowed to enter two designs, each of which must be approved by the Tournament. This precaution prevents an excess of eagles or ducks or dragons in the same parade. When the theme of the parade was "A World of Wonders," the Committee had to make sure the whole globe was equitably represented; only one float could have an English theme, only one could be set in Scotland, only one could take place in Antarctica. When the theme was "A Celebration of Laughter," the Committee had to make certain the half-dozen clowns at least looked different (no easy task).

After the builders' ideas are approved, they go back to the drawing and work on translating those concepts into steel and flowers. How will the acrobatic clown stand on his hands? What's the funniest gag for the rodeo clown? Where will the driver be on the harlequin float? What kind of floral treatment will work best for the court jesters? Even this early in the process, builders need to take decoration into account, for a design must have enough flower-coverage to be favorably considered by the judges. When Rick Chapman was designing Kong this presented a problem: how to make a huge gorilla, which would be covered with palm fiber (*not* flowers), into a floral float. The solutions, Rick explains: "We took Kong back to the island where he was caught, threw out jungle, which is largely green, and decided there must have been an ancient ruin on that island . . . So we built these enormous towers around him that we could put flowers on."

Another challenge the builders face is size. All the floats must pass under a 17-foot freeway bridge during the parade. "One unforgiving concrete structure," Don Bent says, "it makes a real honest man out of you." For New Year's Day, wires come down, telephone cables can be removed, traffic signals are replaced, but nothing can be done about the bridge. Since many floats are oversized, they need to collapse (in less than 25 seconds, according to Tournament regulations) to go under the bridge. This is usually done through animation. "We were doing a simple float, a boat, with a mast," Bill Lofthouse, Don Bent's partner, explained. "The mast had to go up 26 feet to look decent aesthetically. We had to sleeve it down. And by Tournament regulations, it's got to have two animation systems, one back-up, in case anything goes wrong . . . It literally costs us thousands of dollars just to go under that bridge."

The Tournament annually issues a float manual with rules and regulations ("approaching a size that couldn't be contained in the Library of Congress," one builder jokes). It states that all oversized floats—more than 16 feet in height, 18 feet in width, 50 feet in length—must be passed by the Float Variance Committee. The clown that stood 60 feet tall on its hands, King Kong who rose to 34 feet, the Loch Ness Monster who could stretch out 99 feet in length, all needed to be approved. Moreover, their animation systems needed to be tested several times before the parade to be sure they worked. The Variance Committee also has to approve any outwalkers accompanying the floats, any music on them, any more than seven riders on a float, and the use of live animals. Once a live tiger on a float stood up as it was rounding the corner of Colorado and Orange Grove, blocking the driver's view; the top of the float got caught in a traffic signal, stopping the parade for an agonizing 15 minutes. The Committee is cautious about granting variances—at least when it comes to unpredictable members of the animal kingdom.

ANIMATION

Animation not only performs the necessary function of shrinking and expanding a float, it has an aesthetic role as well. "In the early '60s," Bill Lofthouse recalls, "we got a letter from one of the networks that said, 'We could give you a lot more attention if you do something that moves.'" That started a flurry of animated floats, often operated by a kid inside pulling pulleys and levers, making wings flutter, eyes wink or a hand wave. The challenge for the builders was to make these parts move more naturally, not just back and forth like a stick figure on a neon sign, but pivoting in several directions, like a willow in a changing breeze.

This has become possible through hydraulics. With the use of hydraulics, an arm or a leg can move gradually and in several different directions. Builders can make heads that rotate and nod, necks that turn and bend and forearms that pivot at their elbow joints. With one engine pumping over a hundred gallons of hydraulic fluid, a 34-foot gorilla stood up from a crouching position. Initially, the functions were signalled manually, but more and more, as the movement has become more sophisticated, computers give the orders. Now, the insides of some floats look like the cockpit of a 747, with dials, gauges, keyboards, and TV monitors. The highly animated, self-built Cal Poly floats are programmed by a campus computer jock.

In recent years, over half the floats have been animated. There have been genies flying on magic carpets, penguins skating on ice, caterpillars wiggling and inchworms crawling, bears rubbing themselves against trees, and moose munching on grass—looking like animals on the Jungle Cruise at Disneyland. In fact, some of the builders use Disney consultants for their animation. The trouble has been that with so many parts moving on a float, there's a greater risk that something will break down. Many sponsors' contracts penalize a builder thousands of dollars if a float's animation is not functioning properly as it passes the TV cameras. One creative contract specified a fine for each city block a float traveled under tow or with its animation out of order. The builders, recognizing the problem, have recently formed an ad hoc committee with several Tournament representatives to fine themselves for mishaps and breakdowns that foresight could have prevented.

AT THE SITE

The real sculptors of a float are the welders. After the chassis—elongated or shortened or built entirely from scratch—is covered with a steel superstructure, the welders start fashioning steel rods on it. Suddenly a nose takes shape, or a clown's ratty hat appears, or a decorative palm gains a delicate leafy frond. Welders in the float business are artists. "A lot of the time I have to hire artists and teach them to weld," says Don Bent. Sometimes they work from detailed blueprints, but often they have only their eye and an artist's rendering to go by. They create the cheekbones behind a smile and the drapery in a statue and the graceful arch in an Oriental temple. The welders also need to estimate how strong a frame must be to hold the flowers and foliage that will adorn it—flowers and foliage that can triple in weight should it rain on the parade.

On top of the steel goes aluminum screening and chicken wire. Screening (just like what you use on your windows at home) works well to cover joints and small detailed areas. It can be cut, sculpted, and shaped, and when sprayed with polyvinyl "cocooning" it will have a smooth surface appropriate for decorating. For some of the detail work styrofoam is used; it can be cut with a jigsaw, filed, and shaped. Another popular product is Bacarod, flexible foam cylinders that come a half inch to eight inches thick and can be bent, glued, painted, or tied in knots. Bacarod is used for everything from decorative molding to lips and eyebrows. After the float is inspected by the Tournament, the screening and chicken wire are sprayed with the polyvinyl cocooning. Then it is ready to be painted.

Following the artist's rendering and a color scheme worked out in advance, workers paint the floats the colors of the flowers that will cover them. This is done partly in case a flower falls off—the missing pink gladiola petal will not be so noticeable if the surface it was covering is pink. It also gives the kids who decorate the float a paint-by-number grid to follow, to make sure they do not put an orange marigold on a purple dragon. Of course, not just any color will do. The designer has to work out his palette with the floral coordinator. He might want the color of a rare mauve mum, when a purple statice would be much easier to get. He might envision something in salmon, and the floral coordinator shows him a coral gladiola that will do just as well. "Sometimes I have to put the kabosh on a color," concedes floral coordinator Richard Seekins of Charisma Floats. Lou Lujohn, who

79

Float building is an intricate and delicate process. It involves architects, designers, engineers, and a host of volunteers to make it all work.

does the flowers for Festival Artists, is a little more frank, saying, "God only made certain colors."

The colors of the floats are chosen with an eye to their visibility from a distance. "Some colors recede," Richard Seekins explains. "Any dark color recedes after 20 feet and needs to be surrounded by a bright color. Say, if you have a fantasy palm leaf in pink, it needs to be outlined in white for it to read. Or to make blue stand out, you surround it with grey, such as eucalyptus leaves or pods. On the other hand, any earth tones, red, yellows, oranges, carry by themselves." With those colors, Richard likes to add to their vibrancy by playing on slight contrasts. "If I did a red garland all in shades of red, it would be pretty; but instead, I use an orange-red rose, a red carnation, and an orange-red gerbera daisy . . . When two colors next to each other are just a little off, they explode."

FLOWERS . . . AND OTHER NATURAL THINGS

Of course, what makes the Rose Parade the Rose Parade are the flowers, seeds, and foliage on the floats. There can be nothing dyed nor fake. Cleopatra's necklace is threaded with kumquats and cranberries; a bulldog's fur is filled out with thistles and artichokes; the Loch Ness Monster swims in a bed of cabbage, kale, zucchini, and iris. The lion's pelt is made of oatmeal, the German boy's eyelashes are black seaweed, his lederhosen are dusty miller. The matador's golden epaulets are sheaves of wheat, the cobra is made of sharp pinecones. The eagle has shiny red anthurium claws, the fences are made of ironed corn husks, and the boat making its way through the hanging gardens of Babylon has a hull of cattails. Everything in the parade must be covered with something that was once living—flowers, seeds, bark, grass, leaves, fruit, vegetables, spices. About the only item on a Rose Parade float not covered with flowers was the torch from the Statue of Liberty. It rode in the 1986 parade naked in its green oxidized glory.

Recently seeds and spices have been used to glorious effect as skin tones (giving some people cause to complain, "This is not the Tournament of Seeds"). "You're almost a chef when you do a face," says Lotsie Busch Giersch. Decorators cut up dried strawberries and mix them in a blender with cornmeal. Cinnamon and paprika can be added for different shades. Any natural item can be used, if it's crushed, ground, split, smashed, stained—but not dyed—and as long as it retains some of its natural identity.

One substance with serious drawbacks is chili powder; it can leave its handlers burning from their fingers to their toes.

Sometimes items come from odd places. Lotsie once used a clump of mushrooms from her garden in a waterfall on the St. Louis float. Richard Seekins says there's a eucalyptus tree growing near one decorating site that gets pruned every December, whenever the supply of eucalyptus leaves in the decorating tent runs low. One year, Beverly Stansbury, a decorating crew chief, found that no flowers had been ordered for the float she was working on, so she improvised. She borrowed from other floats. She took the discarded yellow centers from poinsettias and used them for one area, the centers of iris for another; out of a rubbish bin she rescued a bushel of orange peels and put them on the float. "One person's trash is another's treasure," she explains. "The best decorated floats come out of trash cans."

Of course, that's not the normal way. The flowers are generally ordered months in advance. Sometimes decorators order directly from a grower, at other times they go through a flower broker. The parade's order at the Los Angeles Flower Mart is considered the largest flower order for a single event. It's estimated that a typical float requires more blossoms than an average florist will buy in five years, as many as 200,000 flowers on one float. Dendrobium orchids come from Hawaii, Singapore,

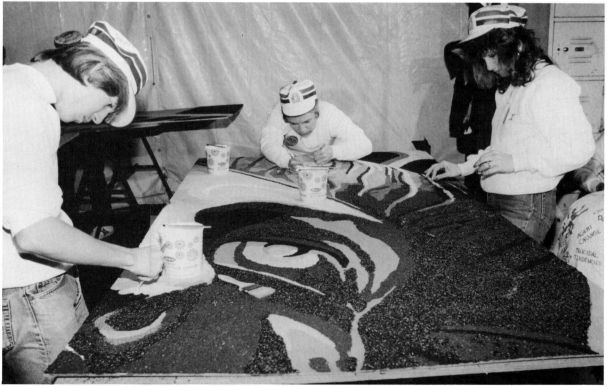

and Thailand; mums from California; carnations from Colorado and Colombia; protea and kangaroo paw from Australia; gerbera daisies, freesias, iris, tulips, and lilies from Holland (which has even named a rose after Pasadena); ranunculus from Africa; anthuriums from Puerto Rico; and roses from California and Colorado. In the first parades, all the flowers came from near Pasadena. Now, nearly fifty percent of them are foreign grown. Finding the correct flowers with the right colors and getting them at the right time is a monumental task. As flower broker Lou Lujohn puts it, "January 2 don't mean nothing to us."

A freeze can ruin a whole crop of carnations, sending builders scrambling to find other sources. Or a shipment from abroad can be quarantined at the airport. Sometimes a crop will produce unexpectedly small blossoms, spoiling a builder's careful calculations. For instance, in 1987, decorators found that a standard bunch of mums covered only two and a half square feet instead of the usual square yard. And one year, Rick Chapman recalled, purple mums were impossible to find because they had all been wiped out by thrips. In the fields where mums are grown, these insects seemed to have skipped all but the purple blooms.

Flowers are delivered to the decorating sites only in the last few days before the parade, and stored in their own tents. When needed, they are prepared for decoration. Mums are cut off their stems, gladiolas are depetaled, roses are put in plastic vials, long-stemmed flowers are wrapped in wire for added support.

By this time the floats are covered with ladders and scaffolding, and T-shirted teenagers crawling all over them like ants, gluing on petals and blossoms. These kids, doing the bulk of the decorating, are usually volunteers from church groups, schools, and clubs. The builders make a modest donation to the organization. And the kids have a lot of fun. "There's often a lot of hand-holding going on," says crew chief Homer Renfrew, "and breaking that up doesn't make the work go any faster, so I tell them to hold two left hands—if they're both right-handed—and keep working."

After a couple of days of decorating, the "petal-pushers," as they are called, become more confident. "I can tell them," Homer says, "'Hey Susie, I need that banner done. Do it the same way it was done on the other side,' or 'Maria and Pat, go up and finish the abbey.'" The teens start taking pride in their craftsmanship, identifying parts of the float they have decorated as "*my* stained glass window" or "*my* bucket" or "*my* star." There are frequent breaks to enjoy fringe benefits from the sponsors, such

---

A typical float requires more blossoms than an average florist will buy in five years, and the flowers come from all over the world. Flowers are delivered the last days before a parade.

as ice cream from Baskin-Robbins or chili from Lawry's. But no one denies it's hard work, and the hours get longer and the labor more frenetic as the floats are readied to receive their most important visitors.

HERE COMES THE JUDGE

Three judges are picked every year to award trophies to the floats in 18 different categories. Some of the categories are very limiting, such as the Founder's Trophy for the most outstanding self-built float. Others offer fine lines of distinction, like the Humor Trophy for humor vs. the Judges' Special Trophy for the most whimsical entry—prompting Ward Kimball, judge of the '86 parade, to decide that humor meant a belly laugh and whimsy was a smile or a smirk. Some are open-ended such as the Tournament Special Trophy, "for exceptional merit not recognized in any other category." But the biggest honor has always been the Sweepstakes Trophy, for the most beautiful float in the parade.

The judges are usually experts in the arts or have a distinguished background in pageantry. Edith Head, Hollywood costume designer; Paige Rense, editor of *Architectural Digest*; Ward Kimball, one of the original Disney animators; Charles Kober of the Los Angeles architectural firm, have all served as judges. The panel also always includes a floral designer or grower whom the builders are usually especially anxious to please. In 1987, when Judge John S. Rowe, an orchid grower, commented on the number of beautiful orchids on floats, the head of the Tournament Judging Committee wryly remarked, "That's because *you're* here."

The judges view the floats three times, twice at the building sites and once in the staging area on Orange Grove Boulevard. On the first visit, two days before the parade, the builders introduce the judges to the floats, pointing out their merits and hinting at their appropriate awards—"This is our candidate for 'small but beautiful'"; "This is our design for 'the most whimsical.'" At the second visit, on the 31st, the builders take down the scaffolding around the nearly completed floats and show them off. They play music and put the float riders on the float, or they take the judges up on catwalks or in lifts to see the floats from the grandstand viewers' perspective. If a float is animated, they will run it, keeping heads bobbing and hands waving. Don Bent goes so far as to cover the floor of the building site with sawdust, to give it an appealing carnival atmosphere. Charles Kober remembers the incongruity of seeing his two female co-judges standing in the

Opposite: Carnation's magnificent effort, "A Garden Full of Wonders."
Top: "Sharing the Joy of the Holidays" was presented by the City of San Bernardino.
Above: Farmer Insurance's "International Showcase."

89

sawdust wearing elegant ankle-length minks.

On New Year's Eve, the judges convene in a closed room at the Pasadena Hilton to make their decisions. They consider style, design, animation, originality, and use of flowers. There's no extra money to the builders for a prize, but as Don Bent says, "The prizes mean everything to the client because they get a little more attention on TV, and a few more seconds mean a little more exposure." With that in mind, the judges deliberate for hours. They make their choices that night before they go to bed, knowing they can change their minds one more time when they view the floats in the parade formation area in the early morning hours of New Year's Day.

ON PARADE

In the pre-parade darkness, next to the magnolias and palms on Orange Grove Boulevard, the floats sit—unlit theaters waiting for their audiences, untested performers about to go on for the first time. They will travel a route that has been followed for decades, commemorating the great events of the year past and the years to come; like "Moment of Anticipation" in 1963, showing two astronauts emerging from a space capsule on the craters of a mum-covered moon. There have been floats of prophetic wishful thinking, such as South Pasadena's 1952 election-year entry, showing an ebullient elephant entering the White House with a dejected donkey exiting out the back. And floats over the years have marked every changing cultural trend; floral figures of The Beatles singing rock and roll music on the Sees' Candies float of 1965; or Valley girls stuck on a freeway traffic jam on Santa Ana's '86 float; or in 1972, FTD's "psychedelic free-form floral configuration," as the newspapers put it, showing the dawning of the Age of Aquarius.

Floats have bid poignant farewells, such as Union Oil's riderless white horse honoring the late humorist Will Rogers in 1936, or Burbank's 1964 entry called "The President Goes to the Prom." It recalled President Kennedy's visit to the city's high school prom held at the Beverly Hilton when the President was staying there. A somber note was added to the design at the last minute—after the President's death—an empty rocking chair. In 1987, the city of Downey planned to salute the space shuttle (parts of which were built there). After the Challenger disaster, Downey made her float a memorial to the shuttle's brave crew. But then in the same parade, the courageous Voyager pilots Dick Rutan and

Jeana Yeager made an unexpected appearance on the Lawry's float, only days after their nine-day, around-the-world flight without refueling, receiving one of the day's biggest ovations.

Who will be next? What act of courage, what memorable event, what folk hero, what legend only now in the making, will be recreated with aluminum screening, chicken wire, polyvinyl, and every flower know to man? And how much bigger and better and more beautiful will builders build floats? Even the earliest newspaper accounts claim that the parade was "the most beautiful ever," but those pioneers who decorated their tallyhos with Cherokee roses from their gardens and paraded down this same street could never have anticipated what was to come. With imaginative designers, adventuresome sponsors, hard-working decorators, spirited volunteers, and awe-filled crowds to watch, there's no telling. Year after year, you can be sure to hear people exclaim, "The floats this year were better than they've ever been." And that will be no exaggeration.

 TROPHIES

Sweepstakes Trophy Most beautiful	
Theme Trophy Most fitting presentation of the Parade theme	
Queen's Trophy Most effective use of roses in decoration	
President's Trophy Best floral presentation	
Grand Marshal's Trophy Most creative design	
Princesses' Trophy Best small float	
Directors' Trophy Excellence of craftsmanship	
Mayor's Trophy Best display of originality	
Pioneers' Trophy Best characterization of the romance of California	
International Trophy Most beautiful entry from outside the territorial limits of the U.S.A.	
Anniversary Trophy Best presentation of life in the U.S.A.	
Governor's Trophy Best city entry	
Founders' Trophy Most outstanding entry in the self-built classification	
Isabella Coleman Trophy Most unusual and unique entry	
Animation Trophy Best display of animation	
Humor Trophy Best display of humor	
Judges' Special Trophy Most whimsical entry	
Tournament Special Trophy Exceptional merit not recognized in any other category	

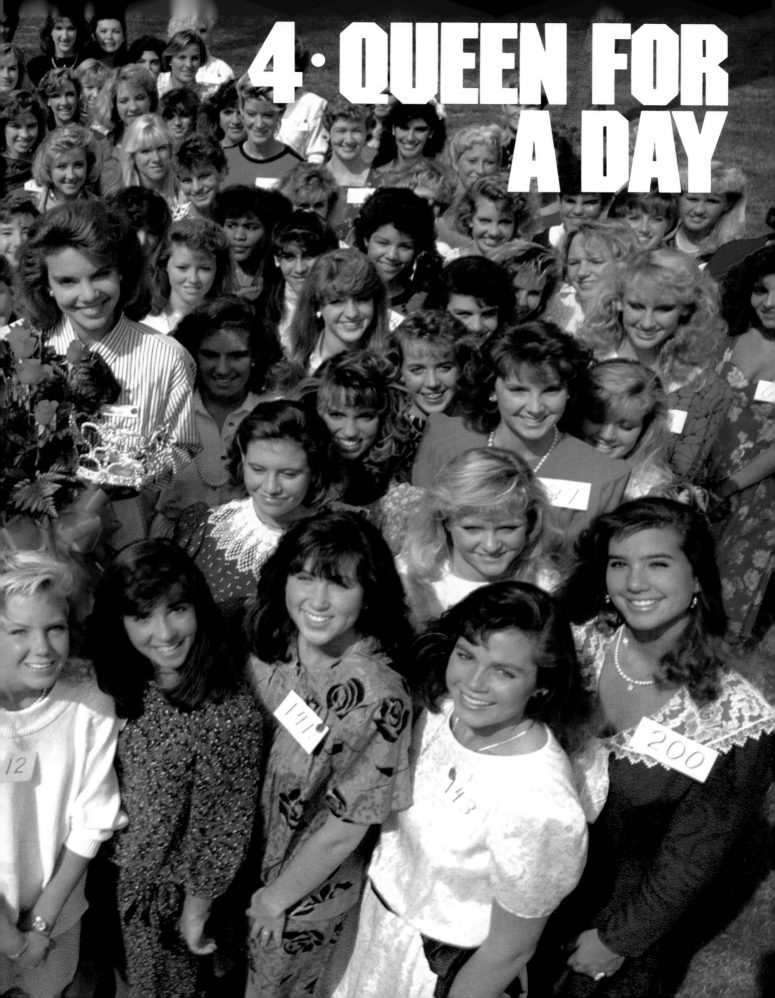

Every January 1, no matter where she is, Dorothy Edwards Conlon is treated like a queen all day. Her husband brings her whatever she wants to her throne, a ringside seat by the TV where she watches the floral parade and Rose Bowl game that day. In 1932 Dorothy Edwards, a cheery-faced brunette from Covina, California, was picked out of her class at Pasadena City College to reign over the Tournament of Roses. Ever since then, "Queen Dot" has been part of a select sorority of Rose royalty, queens and princesses for a day, which hundreds of Pasadena girls vie to join each year.

As early as September, right at the beginning of the school year, the Tournament sends out committeemen and the retiring queen and princesses to talk at local colleges and high schools about auditioning for the court. Any girl who lives in the Pasadena Area Community College District is eligible to try out. She must be at least 17, not over 21, unmarried, a full-time college student or high school senior in the district, and maintaining a "C" average or better. After seeing a short slide presentation telling them what to expect, the girls bombard the Tournament representatives with questions. "Will I have to cut my hair?" "Will I have to get my ears pierced?" "If I don't get selected, can I try out again next year?" "If I get called back, should I wear the same dress?"

The answers are "Probably," "No," "Yes," and "Most girls do." Queen Leslie Kawai '81 remembers wearing her lucky yellow "banana" dress to each session. Queen Suzy Gillaspie '83 wore her same green dress, figuring, "If they saw me in it once they'll remember me when they see me in it again." Queen Katy Potthast '82 was so tired of her lucky, off-white, V-neck dress with its tie-around waist that after becoming queen, she threw it on the floor, resolving never to wear it again.

The judges are Tournament members, the nine white suiters who make up the Queen and Court Committee. Usually around a thousand girls (and an occasional boy, who is automatically disqualified) show up at the first tryout. Combing their hair and touching up their makeup, they wait in the glaring sunshine in the garden at the Tournament House, preparing to meet the judges who sit under an awning with polite smiles on their faces and pencils in hand. Identified only by number, the candidates pass in front of the judges' table, say their number, do a slow turn and walk back. Sometimes a girl will forget the rules and blurt out her name. At other times a judge will decline to score a girl he or she knows. Using a number system (like jurors scoring Olympic

divers) the judges rate the contestants on appearance, poise, personality, smile, speaking ability, and carriage. Looks are important, but it's not a beauty contest—no swimsuits, no evening gowns.

"We're looking for the girl-next-door," the judges say, but they want the rare girl-next-door who can hold her own with well-known celebrities, be articulate on national TV, and smile for more hours than seems humanly possible. Often the girls who try out do it almost as a lark. "I don't know," Queen Suzy says, "since my sisters did it, I figured I'd do it." Queen Ann Marie Colborn '84 admitted, "I'd never really thought about it. It's just what you do when you grow up in Pasadena."

From the first audition, 250 girls are called back, then around 60 for the semi-finals and finally 25 finalists. At these sessions, the young ladies are asked a few questions. "Why do you want to be a princess?" "How did you react to the letter calling you back?" As the numbers get smaller, the questions get harder. "If you had to come back to life as someone else, who would you be?" "If you could interview anyone in history, who would it be?" Privately, the Committee checks up on candidates' academic records and school histories, disqualifying anyone who comes from outside the Pasadena Community College District or who inflates her grade point average. Occasionally the committee consults a makeup or hair advisor to see if a change in hairstyle or makeup will make a big difference. The finalists sign an agreement allowing the Tournament to make any necessary alterations to their hair and makeup to give them the right regal look.

A COURT IN TRAINING

At nine o'clock on a Monday morning in October, the 25 finalists nervously assemble on the steps of the Tournament House. First the names of the girls' schools are read—"from San Marino High School . . ." or "from Flintridge Prep . . ." or "from Pasadena Community College . . ."—followed by the girls' names, one by one, in a process of agonizing suspense. "Will I be next?" the waiting girls wonder. "Or will I have to go back to school this morning and take the French test I couldn't study for?" Finally, all seven members of the court are presented, wearing for the first and last time of their reign dresses of their own choosing. After the crying and hugging die down, they line up in a "left-to-right," an arrangement according to height, and with huge bouquets of roses in their arms, enjoy a moment of glory in front of

Clockwise from top: 1983 Queen Suzy Gillaspie adjusts her crown at her coronation; the Royal Court is announced to the press; Margarethe Bertelson Knoblock, 1960 queen, with 1986 Princess Christine Huff; 1984 Queen Ann Marie Colborn is named to the crown.

Above and opposite: Dorothy Edwards, chosen queen for the 1933 Tournament, "Fairyland in Flowers," was the first queen to be selected under the process which exists today.

the photographers. It's brief, though; there's much work to be done in few days. The lucky seven need to have their wardrobe fitted, take a few lessons in protocol, meet dozens of people, and have a makeup consultation. As a first step they are whisked away to the beauty salon where their hair will be highlighted, cut, curled, and combed—sometimes beyond recognition.

"I burst into tears when I saw my hair," blonde Queen Katy says. "They'd given it a perm with big huge curls and I looked like Shirley Temple." Only later when she saw it combed out did she feel much better. Bill Bell, who did the girls' hair from 1981 to 1987, says there's occasionally some crying at first. "They have a conception of how they look and we don't see them that way at all . . . They need to look like any girl from the Midwest. We want people to say, 'Oh, if I had a daughter who looked like that' . . . Usually, in a day or so, after everyone tells them how great they look, they like it."

One of the stylist's goals is to make sure the girls' looks complement each other. "It's an aesthetic thing," Bell says. One girl's hair cannot be down at her waist while another's is cropped boyishly short. In addition, highlighting is important to bring out the shape of the girls' hair when they are on camera. If it's a cloudy day or they step into the shade, their hair will still pick up the bright tawny California light—or at least it will give that illusion.

To make sure they keep the right look, the girls visit the salon as often as necessary for the next three months. They can drop in before a Tournament event and get whatever they need done at the Tournament's expense: a facial, nails, hair. "One year," Bill recalls, "one of the girls hurt herself in a motorcycle accident. We had a masseuse to help her get back in shape."

The seven girls get a big duffle bag filled with cosmetics courtesy of Avon Products. Recently it has included seven shades of eye shadow, three or four blushes, four or five shades of lipstick, two kinds of mascara, eyeliner, powder, base, contouring shadow, a complete skin-care line, and nail polish. Most of the girls admit that they have never worn much makeup before so Sue Cary-Zens, a professional makeup artist and a princess from the 1974 court, shows them how. She picks the right shades, helps bring out their best features, and advises them on the right makeup to be worn when on camera (no blue eye shadow and nothing incandescent or shimmery). Her goal is for each girl to become her own expert. Sometimes her biggest challenge is to make sure they keep their eyebrows tweezed. "They get lazy," she explains. One year she established the brownie rule—whoever forgot to tweeze had to bring brownies for the rest of the court to the next event.

The court-in-training get etiquette lessons and encouragement from Queen Margarethe Bertelson Knoblock '60, or "the drill instructor" as she is affectionately known. In just one exhausting day of classes, she attempts to "round off any rough edges," as she puts it. She teaches the girls table manners and social protocol and gives them pointers on how to handle the press. ("Always look them in the eye when you're talking to them.") She tells them how to stand (with the shoulders back), how to sit (with one hand over the other in the lap, and *never* with the legs crossed), and how to carry a bouquet of roses ("Cradle them like a baby"). The girls learn to carry their Perrier glasses (a princess drinks nothing stronger) and purses in their left hands so they can shake hands with their right. And, of course, they learn the three basic hand-waving motions that they will need on January 1: "unscrewing a light bulb," "washing a window," and the flat-palmed "stop."

The Tournament purchases the royal wardrobe from a Pasadena department store—for over a dozen years it has been I. Magnin. The girls get one "after five" dress, two blazers, four blouses, two different colored ties, two sweater vests, one sweater, one pair of pants, three skirts, pearls, pearl earrings, gold earrings, three pairs of shoes, one fur wrap, one raincoat, gloves, one ballgown, and one tiara. All the items—except the ballgown, of course—can be mixed and matched to make up to 30 different combinations. Each outfit is coded with a letter of the alphabet, so that "J" might be "argyle sweater, black skirt, yellow blouse, vanilla hose, gold earrings, black bag." The girls are issued a detailed agenda (so complicated it's mapped out by a computer) telling them what ensemble to wear for which event. The only items to be worn at all times are name tags reading "Princess Mary" or "Princess Sandra." Of course the big question still remains: Who will wear the white gown and the rhinestone crown and the only name tag reading "Queen"?

THE FAIREST OF THEM ALL

During the week that the girls are taking etiquette lessons, having their hair done, being fitted for their wardrobe, and generally submitting to being made over, the Queen and Court Committee gets to know them better, looking for the one who should be queen. She needs to have the right combination of regal bear-

ing, California spunk, and girl-next-door looks. She will receive the major focus, becoming the Tournament's leading spokeswoman during her reign. Past queens have been such typical California girls as tennis champ Queen May Sutton 1908, a Pasadenan and the first American woman to win at Wimbledon, or Queen Fay Lanphier 1926, Miss America that year, or Hollywood starlet Queen May McAvoy 1923, who played opposite Al Jolson in the first talkie, "The Jazz Singer." They have been chosen for beauty and charm and sometimes for odd reasons: Queen Virginia Bower Nichols 1949 remembers being selected because the float that year needed a left-handed girl to hold the roses.

Naturally, individual queens have had their fans. Queen Carole Washburn 1961 dated Rose Bowl star Bob Schloredt after the game. Queen Nancy Davis '63 went out with Player of the Game Ron VanderKalen to Dino's on the Sunset Strip after the Bowl. The next day the newspaper carried the story "King and Queen Together for Future Ruling," which amused everybody but her boyfriend. During World War II a small regiment of French soldiers found a colored newspaper picture of Queen Margaret Huntley '49 and wrote to her asking her to be their "Marianne" (an embodiment of the spirit of France). They even went 22 miles to find a typewriter to use for their letters. "Then Hitler crossed the Maginot Line," she recalls, "and I never heard from my French pals again."

These days the queen appears, with or without her court, on the Today Show, the Bob Hope Special, Hollywood Squares, the David Letterman Show. Recently queens have gone to Japan to represent the Tournament in a parade there. The 1986 queen, Aimee Richelieu, made a last-minute trip to Washington, D.C. to meet President Reagan at the signing of the bill making the rose America's national flower. That same year the new court for 1987 made a guest appearance on the Joan Rivers TV show. The queen had not been selected yet, so Rivers asked the girls to close their eyes and raise their hands if they privately thought they would be chosen. When not a hand was raised, Rivers insisted, "Come on, this is America, you have to be proud of yourselves." The second time, all seven raised their hands.

Because the queen is such an important representative of the Tournament, the Queen and Court Committee takes great care in making their decision. To give themselves time to think, they take the girls on a weekend retreat to the beach community of Balboa. While the court makes impromptu appearances at shopping centers and along beachside walks, passing out the

Opposite: Hallie Woods, chosen by her Pasadena High School classmates in 1905, was the Tournament's first queen. She made her own gown.
Below: After a hiatus of two years in which no queen was elected, Ruth Palmer was the choice in 1911.

1906 **Elsie Armitage**

1928 **Harriet Sterling**

1923 **May McAvoy**

1930 **Holly Halsted**

Yesterday's Queens

1935 **Muriel Cowan**

1908 **May Sutton**

1931 **Mary Lou Waddell**

Yesterday's Queens
(continued)

1937 **Nancy Bumpus**

1939 **Barbara Dougall**

1941 **Sally Stanton**

1944 **Naomi Riordan**

1947 **Royal Court**

1946 **Patricia Auman**

1947 **Norma Christopher**

1950 **Marion Brown**

1940 **Margaret Huntley**

ubiquitous Tournament rose stickers, the Committee considers its choices. That Sunday night, they deliberate behind closed doors. After considering conversations, fleeting impressions, and revised assessments, they select the queen. Then for 48 hours their decision is kept secret. No one else knows . . . except the proprietor of a local shoestore. On his shelves he has seven pairs of white satin pumps, six of which will be dyed to match the princesses' ballgowns. The seventh pair, labeled with one girl's name, stays white, waiting like Cinderella's glass slipper for the uncrowned queen.

On Tuesday morning the girls assemble in a "left-to-right" on a small stage in front of the Tournament House. Across from them, with their backs to the sun, photographers stand ready, cameras in hand, gathered in temporary bleachers like fans at an old-style Hollywood premiere. The Tournament President asks for the envelope, "please" (just like at the Oscars), and the name of the new queen is read. Cameras flash, videos roll, tears flow, shrieks fly, everyone hugs the new queen, who suddenly has to speak into a microphone, answering a dozen questions all at once. "What does it feel like being Queen of the Tournament of Roses?" reporters ask. "Did you think you would be selected?" "Were you surprised?" Queen Suzy Gillaspie '83 remembers being taken upstairs afterwards to have her clothes changed—"they have ladies taking off your blouse and putting on your skirt for you"—and she noticed that her whole chest was blotched from a nervous reaction.

Only two days later, the queen is crowned on the lawn outside of the Tournament House. It's outdoor luncheon for over 1,400 people, with the wind blowing through the royal and date palms, the cars of the curious driving slowly by, and the sun so bright many of the guests are wearing dark glasses. Trumpeters in knickers play a fanfare to herald the entrance of the court and the girls walk down a red-carpeted runway smiling to their friends and families. The actual Coronation is a little like the end of the Miss America Pageant. There is an Austrian crystal crown for the queen to wear; there are pre-recorded messages from each of the princesses ("'Shock' is the word I think of to describe my being selected . . ."), quick introductions and gracious acceptance speeches ("in wearing this crown, I take pride in . . ."). Occasionally the girls look like unsure 17-and 18-year-olds when they glance at each other with a look in their eyes that says, "What do I do now?" But somehow the sparkle of the tiaras and crown rule the day. As the girls cradle their bouquets of roses in their gloved hands, the timid smiles disappear and looks of assurance take their place, saying, "Yes, I am a princess" or "I am the queen." When the announcer says, "I now officially present to you the court of the Tournament of Roses," and the news is greeted by a hundred clicking cameras, there is no doubt that the queen and her court are ready to rule their subjects.

ROYAL TOURS

For the next two and a half months the girls' lives are hardly their own. They make almost ninety appearances, carting around their school books with them wherever they go, fulfilling their academic responsibilities as best they can. They attend Rotary lunches, community fund-raisers, father-daughter dinners, open houses, formal dances; they visit hospitals, factories, offices, and retirement homes; they greet teams, visiting dignitaries, parade bands, float builders, and equestrians. And wherever they go, they are chauffeured, escorted, supported, and supervised by the Queen and Court Committee members and their spouses. One helpful member always keeps the "goodie bag," full of emery boards, aspirin, smelling salts, bobby pins, and nail polish to meet any unforeseen emergency. Another holds the tiaras and crown in a wooden, velvet-lined box built especially for the court. All of them take pictures for the girls, dangling a half-dozen cameras from their wrists, labeled "Princess Karen" or "Princess Sandra." During those hectic two months, the Committee and the girls grow exceptionally close, joking together, finding nicknames for each other, gathering stories that they will retell at reunions for years to come.

Many of the events the girls attend are put on by Tournament participants. For instance, Kodak takes them on a tour of their Whittier plant and gives each of them a camera with unlimited film and developing privileges during their reign. (Most girls confess to filling three or four scrapbooks by the time they are done.) Avon hosts a mother-daughter event at their Pasadena headquarters where the girls get to perform makeovers on their mothers. Queen Aimee said it made a difference for her mother. "My mother usually doesn't wear makeup. Now she wears a little eye shadow, a little mascara and if she gets really wild, she'll wear eyeliner."

Perhaps the most fun for the girls is getting to know the football teams. They meet them at the airport, then again at the Beef Bowl at Lawry's Prime Rib restaurant—where the teams get

all the prime rib they can eat—and generally the girls accompany them when they visit Disneyland in between workouts. "Imagine being with both teams at the same time," Queen Carole Cota 1966 said during her reign. "Only a girl can appreciate those odds—80 to 7." Queen Leslie Kawai 1981 remembers it being easy to tell which Michigan guys had been with the girls on the rides at Disneyland. "We had these white angora sweaters and they wore blue blazers. They got all this white fuzz on them." She only regrets that she did not get to know the players very well. "I missed out because I had a boyfriend then. I was very loyal."

When Queen Katy Potthast 1982 met the Iowa team at the airport she was hoisted on the shoulders of quarterback Gordy Bohannon for picture-taking. He looked up at her and said, "My God, you're gorgeous." She blushed suitably. Then at the Beef Bowl with the Washington team, Queen Katy was disappointed that she was seated at the table with the college dignitaries and coaches. "Next time, with Iowa," she told the head of the Queen and Court Committee, "don't sit me at the table with the presidents." Alas, she was seated there anyway; but this time, Gordy Bohannon sat with her. "It was just like it was the two of us. We talked all night."

So began a queen's whirlwind romance with a Big Ten quarterback. Before the game, they went shopping, to a Christmas Eve party together, and almost every night they talked on the phone for hours. When the news leaked out, an AP reporter called up Katy and asked her if she was engaged. "No, I'm not," she coolly responded. Even Iowa coach Haydon Fry teased Gordy. If the quarterback made any errors in practice, Fry suggested, "you've got too many queens on the mind."

THE BIG DAY

Like a bride preparing for her wedding day, the girls never lose sight of the culmination of all their activity, the parade and game on New Year's Day. Several hours before dawn on January 1 they are picked up by members of the Queen and Court Committee and chauffeured to the Tournament House. Passing one barricade after another, they wave at the white suiters who are directing traffic in the parade formation area. The floats are parked on Orange Grove. A giant fish covered in mums, a tiger made out of marigolds, and a moose of coco palm fiber eye the girls warily. The teenaged revelers lining the parade route hardly notice the girls. They are finally falling asleep in their sleeping bags, the

Dolores Brubach, in 1929, was the first of the "War Queens." Because of the war, and for security reasons, the West Coast was "blacked out," the game shifted to Duke University, and the parade cancelled. Queen Dolores and her Court rode down a nearly deserted Colorado Avenue on New Year's Day.

109

embers of their hibachis dying out, the radios turned down, the TVs turned off. The Tournament House seems unnaturally quiet, as though it were the Presidental Palace of some banana republic on the eve of a revolution, the lights ablaze, no one in sight, and all entrances heavily guarded.

Inside the girls are shown upstairs to the Queen and Princesses' Room. Sue Cary-Zens has their makeup spread out on a table—she will need to put some extra color on them today to keep their complexions from washing out in the bright January sunlight. The hairdressing staff works on their hair. The coiffures will have to last to the end of the football game 12 hours later, so the stylists put on an extra coat of heavy hairspray, sometimes so much that their hair looks, in Bill Bell's words, "like a German helmet." The Queen and Court Committee and spouses hover in the background like nervous mothers and fathers of the bride.

The sun comes up slowly that morning. First the sky becomes light above the palm trees and the floats; then sunlight hits the mountains, turning the purple crests gold; finally it warms the streets and crowds moving to find a place to watch the parade. The TVs inside the Tournament House are tuned in to the pre-parade coverage, and the girls put on their taffeta ballgowns right over their sweats and longjohns—after all, the TV interviewer remarks that he can see his breath. The crown and tiaras are adjusted, gloves are pulled on. A few girls have not eaten much breakfast, but no one feels like eating much anyway. In front of the Tournament House, the Today Show wants to ask them just a few questions before they step on (or are hoisted by a forklift) to their float. They are given their bouquets of roses, then they are on their way.

It's a dizzying two-and-a-half hour ride to the end of the parade. Stand after stand of thousands wave at them and call out their names. There are people on top of buildings, people hanging out of windows, people hanging off of trees. The girls wave to friends and family as they pass old landmarks, a store, a church, a school. Queen Ann Colborn, 1984, remembers how odd it was that you could make eye contact with individual people out of so many thousands. A camp counselor during the summer, she especially enoyed waving to her pint-sized campers. "They were always kind of in disbelief, especially seeing me in a dress and a crown. They were used to seeing me in shorts and a ponytail."

At the end of the parade there are several white suiters to help them off the float. The girls are eager to get to a restroom—to take off their longjohns, among other reasons (by now it's 80

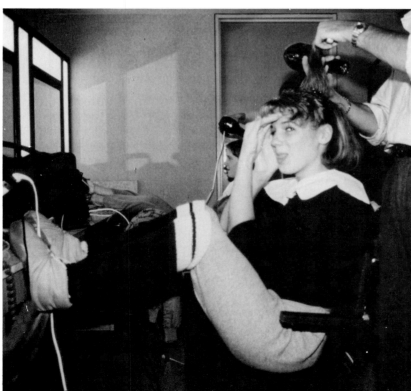

Opposite: 1960 Queen Margarethe Bertelson is crowned by Tournament President Ray Dorn.
Left: Queen Dawn Baker (center left) and Court with Ronald Reagan, then CBS parade announcer.
Below left: 1982 Queen Katy Potthast reacts to her new hairstyle.
Below right: Jimmy Stewart shows 1981 Queen Leslie Kawai the proper wrist action for a wave.

Opposite: Princess Diane Welch gets the royal treatment. Every member of the court gets their hair highlighted, cut, curled, and combed.
Left: 1987 Queen Kristen Harris.
Bottom: Kristen and her Court in the parade.

113

degrees outside). They change into their matching skirts and blazers for the game, and take quick pictures of each other to use up their remaining Kodak film. In the meantime, Sue touches up their makeup. "They get so pale. They've been yelling to friends. They're tired." Then they are chauffeured one last time, escorted by a police motorcade to the Rose Bowl, the sirens blaring, all cars moving aside to let them pass. After lunch, the girls make a grand entrance into the Bowl sitting in the back of a vintage Stutz or a Packard, waving to still more thousands of people. Seated in 50-yard-line seats, they watch the game, still smiling as much as possible (the camera is still on them), sometimes pinching each other to stay awake . . .

Then all too soon it's over. As Queen Leslie Kawai 1981 recalled, "all of the sudden the Committee says, 'Okay, we'll help you find your parents.' And then you're stuck in traffic with your parents and everybody else." Back to school, back to the books, back to T-shirts and jeans, back to paying to have a haircut, back to wearing just as much or as little makeup as you please, back to anonymity.

Queen Suzy Gillaspie remembers being happy when it was all over. "You're so ready to sit back and be yourself. Then you had to be Polly Perfect, and always 'on'" She laughs. "Never in my life would I like to be Princess Di!" Queen Katy Potthast also admits there was no letdown on January 2. "I was so exhausted, it was a relief. I don't think I did anything all day." The letdown, if it comes, comes later. As Queen Pamela De Tedesco 1970 said at a recent reunion of queens, "You learn that everything in life can't be that glamorous." Queen Suzy agrees. She was not impressed when she saw herself on the cover of the *Los Angeles Times* the day after the parade. "Now I look at it and it's like, 'Wow.' . . . Then I was in a different world."

Queens have gone on to careers in film, TV, and on Broadway. Queen Cheryl Walker '38 was in the popular vintage film "Stage Door Canteen." Queen Naomi Riordan '44 was the ingenue in the play "Country Girl." Recent Queens Suzy, Katy, and Leslie have all made a number of TV commercials. Past queens have become teachers, models, singers, housewives, students, secretaries, dancers, writers, exercise teachers, voice teachers, etiquette teachers, makeup consultants. They get together with their courts at weddings, showers, and mini-reunions. Those who live far from Pasadena generally host a party in front of their TV sets every New Year's Day. And every year the queens get together at the annual Kodak Queens' Brunch.

There they reminisce, gossip, meet the press, share pictures of children and grandchildren, compare health. "I am glad she appears so healthy," one queen from the '40s said, eyeing a queen from the '30s at the brunch. "I am not anxious to become known as the oldest living queen of the Tournament of Roses." The most important thing is to welcome the new queen. "They're part of your sorority and you're part of theirs," says one queen. After all, they know what it's like to ride in the parade, to keep your hands away from your face as you pass the press boxes, to smile for so many hours you forget how to frown, to receive letters from Singapore and Sydney and Taipei, to flirt with a hundred football players, to take more pictures than you could ever put in a scrapbook, to have more pictures taken of yourself than you'll ever see, to wave to thousands, to be the center of everything on one spectacular day . . . to be the Queen of the Tournament of Roses.

Past queens' reunion. Maiden names are in parentheses. Seated, l-r: Marilyn (Smuin) Martell, 1955; Margaret (Huntley) Main, 1940; Dorothy (Edwards) Conlon, 1933; Kristen Harris, 1987; Holly (Halsted) Balthis, 1930; Joan (Culver) Warren, 1956; Norma (Christopher) Winston, 1947; Leah (Feland) King, 1953; Sally (Stanton) Rubsamen, 1941. Standing, l-r: Ann (Mossberg) Hall, 1957; Kathleen (Arnett) Miller, 1971; Robin (Carr) Christensen, 1975; Nancy (Thorne) Skinner, 1952; Miranda (Barone) Clinco, 1974; Margarethe (Bertelson) Knoblock, 1960; Aimee Richelieu, 1986; Barbara (Schmidt) Mulligan, 1954; Salli (Noren) Throop, 1973; Ann (Martin) De Unamuno, 1976; Leslie Kawai, 1981; Catherine (Gilmour) Garfield, 1979.

115

5 · GRAND MARSHALS, HORSES AND BANDS

Only a few celebrities have ever been asked to serve as grand marshal of the Tournament of Roses twice, one of whom was Bob Hope. "They picked me to be grand marshal because they wanted a movie star and the uniform wouldn't fit Lassie," the dapper comedian quipped in 1947. "This will be my first game from a 50-yard-line seat. Last year I had a dollar ticket . . . I was 86th in line for the telescope at Griffith Observatory." His association with the Tournament continued over the years with annual appearances by the Rose Queen and Court on his TV special, and by the time he returned to lead the parade in 1969, he looked older and wiser. But that year the jokes were on him.

Trouble began when he showed up at Tournament House an hour late. There was a hurried awards ceremony—during which a stranger unexpectedly presented him with a golf putter. Then Hope got into his car, a Chrysler convertible, equipped with a radio transmitter and receiver so he could greet the world as he passed the TV cameras, and a portable TV so Hope could watch the Bowl games played earlier in the day. Not surprisingly, the car would not start. The overtaxed battery was dead.

An intrepid white suiter drove up with a jumper cable and got the car going, and the parade was underway. All went well for about an hour, when the car died again on Colorado Boulevard, and no one could start it. A truck driver offered to push it. A tow truck offered to pull it. At the last moment five scruffy teens (they would have been called "hippies" back then) volunteered their help. Ah, the indignity of seeing the glorious Chrysler, a company

118

for which Hope was then the national spokesman, being pushed by some barefooted, long-haired youth! But what else could Hope do?

The kids pushed for two miles, even uphill on Sierra Madre Boulevard, with Hope good-humoredly waving his golf putter over their heads as though it were a whip and they were Roman galley slaves (à la *Ben Hur*). Dorothy Lamour, Rosemary Clooney, and Barbara Eden riding on the float ahead of him (aptly named "Thanks for the Memories" for Hope's theme song) looked on in amusement. At the end of the route, Hope gave the kids his tickets to the Bowl, telling several surprised Tournament officials, "You'll find me other seats to the game." But the biggest surprise was in store for the dignitaries seated next to the "galley slaves." "Where did you get your tickets?" they were warily asked.

"Bob Hope gave them to us."

HORSES AND RIDERS

None of this would have happened if Hope had traveled the original way of the grand marshals, on horseback. Clearly, that's where the term "grand marshal" came from, when local horsemen, like the elegant M.S. Pashgian, *marshaled* the parade in jodphurs, a top coat, and a top hat. A pageant that started out in 1890 obviously depended on horsepower for many years. Even when cars were first introduced they were relegated to the rear so they would not frighten the jittery horseflesh. Moreover, engines overheated and cars broke down (like Hope's), but horses always finished. Even today, when half-a-dozen floats might have mechanical failures, the St. Louis entry pulled by the Anheuser-Busch Clydesdales has never failed to reach Victory Park at the end of the route. But the Clydesdales are now the exception. After 1920, when nearly all floats were engine-powered, parade horses were no longer beasts of burden. They are there for show.

And what a show it is! In the parade today there are Appaloosas, pintos, palominos, Friesians, mustangs, exotic Bashkir Curlies, workaday mules—everything from the hefty Clydesdales, which weigh about a ton apiece, to the diminutive miniatures, which stand no taller than a man's waist. A few celebrated race horses have ridden along Colorado Boulevard, such as the popular Malicious in 1940, but racing thoroughbreds need to save their strength for their afternoon furlongs at Santa Anita. Stuart and Susie Hamblen ride Peruvian horses, rare descendants of the horses Pizarro first brought to the New World.

They walk with a peculiarly smooth gait, the *paso*, so smooth in fact you can ride them carrying a glassful of champagne without spilling a drop.

For many years equestrian entries in the parade were restricted to Western riders in Western attire with Western saddles and tack. Today the mixture is more eclectic. There are of course the spectacular polished silver saddles, trappings, and tack from Ed Bohlen's in Burbank, long-time suppliers to Hollywood cowboys like Gene Autry, Bill Boyd (Hopalong Cassidy), and Rex Allen. But equestrians also dress in burnouses and djibbas appropriate for the Arabian horses they ride, or Spanish serapes on Andalusians and Peruvian ponchos on Peruvians. And the ladies riding sidesaddle are in proper Victorian attire—reminiscent of the pre-1893 parades, before equestriennes were permitted to wear bifurcated skirts.

Some equestrians have worn what are obviously costumes: Zorro in his cape, the Lone Ranger with his mask, Ken Maynard dressed up as Buffalo Bill, Fort Huachuca's B Troop of the 4th US Cavalry Regiment in their 1880s Army uniforms. Or take the Long Beach Mounted Police, a presence in the parade for nearly 40 years. If they look less than ferocious in their rhinestone-studded shirts and silver gun belts, it's because they are not real policeman, but honorary ones deputized for the occasion.

The Indians are more authentic in their dress. Iron Eyes Cody (who got his name from wearing eyeglasses as a child) rides in his beaded buckskins with his black braids framing his stolid face. He is joined by his comrade, Jim Whitecloud, who is half Creek and half Oneida. Whitecloud wears his father's impressive eagle-feather headdress with its red-fluff tips. In his hand he carries a ceremonial feather-covered lance which he raises to the crowds.

The horses themselves have often been important personalities, such as the Lone Ranger's Silver. Roy Rogers and Dale Evans rode Trigger and Buttercup along Colorado Boulevard for many years before the horses went to their reward—preserved by the taxidermist's art and now on display at the Rogers' Victorville museum. Leo Carrillo mounted his beloved pinto Sui San and his palomino Conquistadore in countless parades. Veteran rop spinner Montie Montana has ridden Rex, Comanche, Spot, Apache, Pancho, Danny, Larry and Governor since his first Tournament in 1932.

Getting a horse ready for the parade can take days. Their thick winter coats need to be clipped, washed, and combed. Their horseshoes are coated with barium to prevent slipping on Colo-

Opposite: Television star Leo Carillo ("Oh, Pancho!"), a parade fixture for years, aboard his beloved Conquistadore.
Above: Equestrian M.S. Pashgian, grand marshal in 1915, the last year of the chariot races.

rado's asphalt. The manes and tails are combed out, brushed and washed, and sometimes bleached or braided. Often their hooves are covered with glue and then dusted with glitter to pick up the sunlight. Newscaster George Putnam says it takes him four days to polish his silver saddle, leggings, trappings, and tack. The silver he wears weighs 185 pounds, not to mention the silver on his horse. He found out how heavy that was one New Year's morning when he got off his horse to help a colleague, and then could not get back on. Now he waits till *after* he mounts to put on the silver.

George Putnam, "Dean of the West," as he calls himself, is an example of the sort of legendary horseman the Tournament has attracted over the years. Known for his TV and radio shows, "One Reporter's Opinion" or "Talk Back," Putnam is invariably greeted with his slogan: "See you at ten," the crowd yells. "See you then," he responds. Over the years, a ritual has developed. There is always one fellow at the end of the route who throws him an apple. On Sierra Madre, someone always holds up a springer spaniel to him, a dog Putnam rescued when it was lost on the parade route a dozen years ago. "Hey George, haven't you gained some weight?" bystanders ask. "Hey, how do you keep your gut in?"—kidding he takes good-naturedly. And you always know that, as sure as the happy ending to an old Western, he will be there next year.

Like him, Montie Montana is another Rose Parade legend. After over 55 years of Tournaments, nothing seems to age him. He spins his lariat above his head tirelessly for the entire 5½ miles, sending it out to catch delighted bystanders. For 30 parades he has roped Baptist preacher James Widcomb Brougher in front of the Pasadena Elks Club. Parents hold up their youngsters to him and say, "Rope him. You roped me when I was his size." He has roped Don Drysdale, Roy Rogers, Ronald Reagan, and President Eisenhower. In his special Bohlen's saddle, he prances from side to side, his arm always in motion. His horse is wary of the brick crosswalks in front of the Pasadena Plaza, and was not happy walking across a large rose painted on the asphalt, but nothing stops Montie. "With all the excitement," he says, "I don't get tired until the next day."

GRAND GRAND MARSHALS

Some of the finest equestrians have also been grand marshals: Roy Rogers and Dale Evans in 1977, L. A. Sheriff Eugene

GRAND MARSHALS

GRAND MARSHALS

Opposite: President Dwight
D. Eisenhower with Queen
Nancy Kneeland and
Princess Diana Duval.
Top left: Roy Rogers and
Dale Evans, grand marshals
in 1977.
Top Right: Chief Justice Earl
Warren in 1955.
Left: The Richard Nixon
family, in 1953. Nixon, like
Bob Hope, was grand
marshal twice.

123

Sometimes horse and rider share equal billing, as did Clayton Moore and Silver (opposite) in 1987. Getting a horse ready for the parade can take days. Horses need to be washed, combed and clipped, and their shoes coated with barium to prevent slipping on asphalt.

Biscailuz in 1937, and most notably Leo Carillo. Dressed in the costume of a California don, Carillo led the parade in 1938. Claiming a lineage back to the early days of Spanish California, he made parades a particular cause of his—as though they were the reincarnation of Spanish Fiestas on the Old Ranchos, as he once claimed. For generations, even after serving as grand marshal, he *was* the Rose Parade, zigzagging back and forth between the blue honor lines to greet the crowds, tossing confetti to the grandstands, and smiling the friendly, mustachioed grin that made him one of Hollywood's favorite good-hearted bad men. From an actor who impersonated Chinese, Italians, and Mexicans, there seemed nothing incongruous about his explanation of the confetti. "It's an old Spanish custom," he said.

He could just as easily have said, "It's an old Tournament custom that the grand marshal be a Republican." Carillo was one. So were many other notable grand marshals: Richard Nixon, Herbert Hoover, Dwight Eisenhower, Earl Warren, Gerald Ford, Everett Dirksen, Charles Wilson (known for his phrase "What's good for General Motors . . .").

Two of these Republicans served twice: Earl Warren and Richard Nixon. Earl Warren had the honor as governor of California in 1943, when there was no parade due to the War; he returned in 1955 as the newly appointed Chief Justice of the Supreme Court. Richard Nixon was grand marshal (or "Grand marshall" as it was spelled on his car) first in 1953, a substitute for President Eisenhower who backed out because of the pressures of his imminent inauguration. He returned again in 1960, in the midst of his own campaign for the Commander in Chief's spot. That campaign did not go too well, but perhaps to prove there were no hard feelings against Pasadena, he made an unofficial visit to the Bowl in 1969, just before assuming residency in the White House.

Other grand marshals have been military heroes. Admiral Sims had the honor in 1934, when it rained 12 inches in 48 hours and Sims declared, "I'm going to lead the parade if I have to swim every inch of the way." Admiral Halsey was at the helm in 1946, the first parade after the War, and Halsey said, "I thought about all those other New Year's Days—the tough ones—that led up to this." There were seven Congressional Medal of Honor winners in 1952, three Apollo astronauts in 1972, General Omar Bradley in 1948, Captain Eddie Rickenbacker in 1957, and one of the few surviving Civil War drummers in 1928. Dwight Eisenhower proved to be a difficult military man, and politician, to get. He

Opposite: 1966 grand
marshall Walt Disney with
leader of the parade. Disney
agreed to marshal only if
allowed to bring a number
of his characters to cavort
with him. Left: 1940 Queen
Margaret Huntley with grand
marshals Charlie McCarthy
and Edgar Bergen.

agreed to lead the parade in 1951, but because of the escalating conflict in Korea he was called back into service and passed the honor on to a little-known corporal recently wounded in the war. Hurriedly released from the hospital at Camp Pendleton, Corporal Bob Gray put his injured arm in a diaper for a sling (borrowed from the maternity ward) and was launched into Rose Parade stardom. "Tomorrow," he admitted, "I'm going to be Joe Blow Nobody again."

Ever since America's Sweetheart Mary Pickford led the 1933 parade, Hollywood has proved to be a fruitful source of grand marshals. Shirley Temple served in 1939, wearing a big red badge almost as tall as she was. Edgar Bergen brought Charlie McCarthy to Pasadena for the parade of 1940; he was so tired afterwards from smiling (woodenly?) he was placed in a trunk for days. Kate Smith sang "God Bless America" at the Bowl in 1976 (eclipsing an earthquake— measuring 4.2 on the Richter scale— that rocked Southern California earlier in the day). In 1966, Walt Disney rode in a car surrounded by his characters. In 1977, the King of the Cowboys and the Queen of the West, grand marshals Roy Rogers and Dale Evans, forewent their usual mounts and rode in a $115,000 gold-plated Stutz d'Italia.

The Tournament Presidents can be unblushingly awed and charmed by their grand marshals. For them, it's a unique

opportunity to hobnob with a celebrity. "Half the time I was 'Boyle,'" says James Boyle, Jr. of his association with his 1985 grand marshal Lee Iacocca, "but at the end of the parade it was 'Jim.'" 1980 President Frank Hardcastle said of his grand marshal Frank Sinatra, "We're two Franks from New Jersey," as though not much had happened to either of them since they both left their native state. Lorne Green and 1980 President Millard Davidson learned they shared the same audiologist; Jimmy Stewart and 1982 President Hal Coombs compared hearing aids. Even a certain complicity can develop between the white suiters and their special guests.

The second time Earl Warren was grand marshal, in 1955, it rained throughout the parade. Elmer Wilson, Tournament President that year, suggested they stop off at C. Lewis Edwards's house on their way to the pre-game lunch to warm up. They did, took off their damp clothes, sat by the fire, and had a drink. "Well, we can't go on one," said Warren, so they had another. "Now we were really getting warm, inside and outside," Wilson remembered, "so we had a third drink." By the time they got to Brookside for lunch, the FBI and seemingly half of the US government was on the lookout for the missing Chief Justice of the Supreme Court. "There wasn't a soul who knew where he was," recalled Wilson. "They certainly tore me apart on that one."

The grand marshals inevitably leave their mark long after they have left Pasadena. On a tour of Wrigley Mansion, white suiters will unabashedly point out where Danny Kaye charmed Tournament guests or where Jimmy Stewart sat at the end of the long day, saying half to himself, "marvelous, marvelous," or where Lee Iacocca nonchalantly did his morning crossword puzzle. Their signed pictures fill the house and offices like the celebrated signatures in the cement in front of Hollywood's Grauman's Chinese theater. And in the Tournament House, just below the stairs, there is a small powder room that will forever be known for a former President and five-star general, Commander of the European forces during World War II. "That's the bathroom where Eisenhower got locked in before the parade in '64," they say. It's still the Eisenhower commemorative loo.

BANDS ACROSS THE NATION

When a high school band marches in the Tournament, they do not march alone. There might be 150 instrumentalists, a dozen flag bearers, sign bearers, baton twirlers, a drum major, and

Opposite: It can take four days to get a saddle and all its trappings polished for the parade. The gear can weigh almost 200 pounds.
Above: Iron Eyes Cody, most famous as the crying Indian in the "Keep America Beautiful" television ad.

129

band director parading down Colorado Boulevard, but they have numerous invisible companions: the band boosters from back home. These tireless parents, teachers, and friends raised the money to get them there. They sponsored bake sales, ice cream socials, car raffles, and barbecues; they organized swap meets, rummage sales, bottle drives, and newspaper drives; they buttered miles of submarine sandwiches, flipped millions of flapjacks and ironed the creases in all those pants. It is impressive enough when a large high school can raise the estimated $500 to $700 per student necessary to send their band out to Pasadena; it is nothing short of amazing when a small town like Newton, Illinois, population 4,000 makes the trip on a chartered train with 245 band members, 325 teachers and parents, and another 530 residents as they did in 1984. That's a fourth of the total population of Newton! And such support is typical of the bands that march in the parade, year after year.

For the 22 bands in the parade, making that five-and-a half-mile trip is like being in the Olympics or qualifying for the Indianapolis 500 (or playing in the Rose Bowl). Every year, some 300 bands apply, sending in pictures, tapes, video tapes, and comments from the contests they have won. Several of those 22 berths are unofficially reserved for a few regulars: the Pasadena Community College Lancer Band, the Salvation Army, the US Marine Corps, McDonald's All-American Band, and the Los Angeles All-City Band. The others are open to the top applicants from across the country, and the world.

The 157 Marching Koalas flew all the way from Newcastle, Australia—their air fare was the biggest expense in the two-thirds of a million dollars they spent to be in the parade. The band from Conroe, Texas, drove in buses, with a police escort leading the way. Band director Michael Nakasone's group from Pearl City High School in Hawaii has made the trip twice, once with 389 members, one of the largest groups ever to play in the parade. The Royal Jordanian Armed Forces Band was an unexpected delight in 1987. The same year, the Noto Youth Marching Band from Suzu City, Japan, marched to the Gojinjo-Daiko cadence, a legendary drumbeat once used to frighten away enemies.

No matter what distances they must travel, raising the money to get to Pasadena is always a challenge. The fundraising projects are clever and diverse. In 1981, a band from Spokane, Washington, cleaned ashes off of roofs (for a fee) following the Mt. St. Helens eruption. In 1976, the John Marshall High School Band of San Antonio, Texas, solicited donations by playing continu-

Mary Pickford and Queen Dorothy Edwards. "America's Sweetheart" in 1933 was the first female grand marshal, as well as the first Hollywood star, to serve as the parade's figurehead. She rode in a coach drawn by four white horses.

ously at a local shopping mall for 52 hours and two minutes, a record at the time. The Pearl City Band Boosters barbecued 47,000 "huli" chickens; Washington, D.C.'s Cardozo High School students sold roses at Redskin football games; several bands have held haunted houses (donations suggested) for Halloween. Almost all have benefit concerts in the spring, often attended by the Tournament President and his wife.

My parents' visit to Monticello, Minnesota (population 3000), is a good example. During their two-day visit they were treated like visiting royalty, feted at a Chamber of Commerce luncheon, toasted at a Band Boosters ice cream social, written up on the front page of the city's newspaper. But the height of their visit was the band's "Prism Concert," during which the band members and director David Thielman promised to knock Dad's socks off. They did, too. Seated in the middle of the auditorium, Mom and Dad were thrilled when suddenly the marching band surrounded them from all sides blaring, "California, Here I Come." I do not doubt Dad's eyes were tearing over, but just as proof of the band's promised success, Thielman brought him a present when Monticello arrived in Pasadena. "Mr. Hamlin," he said, "you left these back in Monticello. Your socks."

CONDITIONED RESPONSE

It takes more than just money to be a success on Colorado Boulevard. Besides needing good musicianship and a hardy embouchure, band members must be in top physical shape for the march. At Monticello, an athletic trainer set up a varied program of running and weight-lifting for the players (especially for those carrying heavy xylophones and Sousaphones). Some compare getting in shape for the parade to training for a marathon. "You need leather lips and leather lungs," says one trombonist. "Marching for several weeks, you build up your endurance, going from 2 miles, to 3, to 4, up to 6 . . . They may say 5 ½ miles, but it's more like 7½ by the time you go from bus to parade and then back to the bus."

Comfortable shoes would seem to be a prerequisite, but

the 1987 band from Holland, Michigan, impressed the crowds by marching in wooden shoes the whole way. The night before they soaked their clogs in water, to prevent cracks, and in the parade each player wore up to eight pairs of socks. This regime must have worked because they suffered few casualties. My mother has never failed to admire the Salvation Army timbrelists. Playing their tambourines, they march the entire route in black pumps with heels at least 1½ inches high (and no holes in the toe and no bows). Margaret Arnold, the director of the timbrelists, tells her charges in September, "Whatever shoes you plan to wear in the Rose Parade, start wearing them now." They need to fit like an old glove.

The Salvationists have been in the parade since 1920, longer than any other band. For years, parade crowds have enjoyed singing along to the hymns they play: "The Old Rugged

Clockwise from top right: Composite US Marine Corps Band; Holland High School Band (note wooden shoes); Pasadena Area Community College District Tournament of Roses Honor Band; Salvation Army; Los Angeles Unified School District All-City Band; Royal Jordanian Armed Forces Band.

133

Above: 1939 Grand Marshal Shirley Temple. When told by her parents that she could marshal, Temple reportedly replied, "Goodie! Will I get to wear a badge?" Did she ever.
Opposite: Pasadena Area Community College District Tournament of Roses Honor Band leads the new Tournament of Roses logo.

Cross," "Battle Hymn of the Republic," "This Is My Father's World," "Rock of Ages" (a little too slow for marching, but it works well when they are stopped behind a stalled float). Other groups play tunes that relate to their hometowns: "Waltzing Matilda" from the Australian Koalas, "Tip Toe Through the Tulips" from Holland's band, "Chattanooga Choochoo" from the John Overton High School band from Nashville, Tennessee, "Hilo March" from the Pearl City group. Sometimes bands use tunes that complement the parade theme: "You've Got to Have Friends" for "Friends and Neighbors," a cartoon medley for "A Celebration of Laughter," Beethoven's "Ode to Joy" for "Rejoice!" Or they will comment on the weather. Fortunately, "The Sunny Side of the Street" and "Don't Rain on My Parade" have all proved perfectly appropriate.

Several of the regular bands are composites, drawing upon the membership of more than one school, or in the case of the Salvation Army, one church. The 300 members of the L.A. All-City Band are the best instrumentalists from 49 different Los Angeles high schools, rehearsing on weekends in the Dodger Stadium parking lot. The McDonald's All-American High School Band is made up of two musicians from each state, wearing their own uniforms with gold (as in the Golden Arches) vests over them. The Pasadena Community College band includes top high school musicians from the college district. Since 1929, they have been the official Tournament of Roses Honor Band, a title they gained for representing the non-Pac-10 teams in the Rose Bowl (which they did until 1946). The only awkwardness came about when an all-white Alabama team in the 1930s threatened not to play on the same field where "their" PCC band, which had one black member, marched. According to Lancer Band archivist Bryant Duffy, in the end, both team and band played, with *all* their members.

PCC has practiced their marching on the Santa Anita parking lot and uncompleted sections of local freeways. Others find parks, shopping mall parking lots, dead-end streets, and if necessary, heated field houses. Compared to the complicated formations most of these groups make in a normal halftime show (and during Band Fest), marching in the parade is easy. If they have a front rank of nine players, the fifth column simply follows the rose line down the parade route, with all other columns marking their positions from that center line. The biggest challenge is the 110-degree (or perhaps 115-degree) turn at Orange Grove and Colorado, a particularly vulnerable spot because that is where the TV cameras are. Duffy remembers one year when a

few Lancers decided to paint marks on the asphalt to guide them through the turn.

On the evening of the 31st, they went up to the corner carrying cans of black glossy paint. Making their way gingerly through the traffic, they were immediately spotted by some policemen. "What are you doing?" they were asked. "We're from NBC," the Lancers quickly lied, "We need to paint some camera cues." With that, the ever-helpful Pasadena policemen stopped traffic and the Lancers painted nine black glossy arrows. When I asked Duffy, who was in the front rank of trombonists, if the arrows helped any, he admitted, "We never found them. We were too scared to look."

AMERICA'S BANDSTAND

Too scared, too excited, or maybe just in awe. No matter how many times you play, ride, or march in the Rose Parade, it's thrilling to round the corner at that 110-degree (or 115-degree) turn and look downhill at a ribbon of floats, horses, and bands in the midst of people, people as far as the eye can see. The old pros recognize the halfway point; they look for cooling drinks from the crowd whenever they stop. They save some energy for going under the Foothill Freeway Bridge, where their brassiest number is deafening to play—like listening to a stereo tuned up all the way, with no neighbors to complain. The novices have been so well prepared, they could probably march the five and a half miles back to where their buses let them off at dawn.

They visited Disneyland and Knotts Berry Farm, they waded in the Pacific, and they celebrated New Year's (if their band director was smart, he had them celebrate at 9:00 or 10:00 as though they were still on Eastern Standard Time or Central Time). Then they got up at 3:00 or 4:00 a.m., ate quick breakfasts on nervous stomachs, rode in buses from their hotels in Anaheim (near Disneyland) or Newport (near the beach) or Inglewood (near the airport), parked at the dead end of the unfinished Long Beach Freeway, walked uphill to their pre-parade positions, and waited. At first it seemed as though the parade was passing them by—the floats, the grand marshal, the equestrians. But then came their turn, and for two hours they were not only in the Rose Parade, they felt like they *were* the parade. The tired lips and lungs, the crowds 20 or 30 people deep, the grandstands that sang along . . .

Nothing was quite like the Rose Parade.

TOURNAMENT OF ROSES GRAND MARSHALS

1890 Dr. Francis F. Rowland	**1924** Col. George S. Parker	**1954** Gen. William F. Dean
1891 none	**1925** Lewis H. Turner	**1955** Earl Warren
1892 Dr. Francis F. Rowland	**1926** Col. L.J. Mygatt	**1956** Charles E. Wilson
1893 none	**1927** Dr. C.D. Lockwood	**1957** Eddie Rickenbacker
1894 Dr. Francis F. Rowland	**1928** John McDonald	**1958** Robert Gordon Sproul
1895 Dr. H.H. Sherk	**1929** Marco Hellman	**1959** E.L. "Bob" Bartlett
1896 Edwin Stearns	**1930** James Rolph	**1960** Richard M. Nixon
1897 Edwin Stearns	**1931** Gen. C.S. Farnsworth	**1961** William F. Quinn
1898 Martin H. Weight	**1932** William May Garland	**1962** Albert D. Rosellini
1899 Martin H. Weight	**1933** Mary Pickford	**1963** Dr. William H. Pickering
1900 Charles Daggett	**1934** Adm. William S. Sims	**1964** Dwight D. Eisenhower
1901 Charles Daggett	**1935** Harold Lloyd	**1965** Arnold Palmer
1902 C.C. Reynolds	**1936** James V. Allred	**1966** Walt Disney
1903 C.C. Reynolds	**1937** Eugene Biscailuz	**1967** Thanat Khoman
1904 Dr. Francis F. Rowland	**1938** Leo Carrillo	**1968** Everett Dirksen
1905 Dr. Francis F. Rowland	**1939** Shirley Temple	**1970** Apollo 12 Astronauts:
1906 John B. Miller	**1940** Edgar Bergen	Alan L. Bean, Charles Conrad,
1907 Dr. Ralph G. Skillen	and Charlie McCarthy	Jr., Richard F. Gordon, Jr.
1908 Dr. Ralph G. Skillen	**1941** E.O. Nay	**1971** Rev. Billy Graham
1909 Walter S. Right	**1942** Kay Kyser	**1972** Lawrence Welk
1910 Dr. Charles F. Holder	**1943** Earl Warren	**1973** John Wayne
and Dr. Francis F. Rowland	**1944** Alonzo Stagg	**1974** Charles M. Schulz
1911 Dr. Ralph G. Skillen	**1945** Herbert Hoover	**1975** Henry L. "Hank" Aaron
1912 E.H. Groenendyke	**1946** Adm. William Halsey	**1976** Kate Smith
1913 Leigh Guyer	**1947** Bob Hope	**1977** Roy Rogers and Dale Evans
1914 Charles Daggett	**1948** Gen. Omar Bradley	**1978** Gerald Ford
1915 M.S. Pashgian	**1949** Perry Brown	**1979** Lathrop K. Leishman
1916 Dr. Francis F. Rowland	**1950** Paul G. Hoffman	**1980** Frank Sinatra
1917 Dr. C.D. Lockwood	**1951** Cpl. Robert S. Gray	**1981** Lorne Green
1918 Dr. Z.T. Malaby	(for General Eisenhower)	**1982** Jimmy Stewart
1919 Frank Hunter	**1952** Medal of Honor Heroes:	**1983** Merlin Olsen
1920 Frank G. Hogan	Lt. Adams, Capt. Harvey,	**1984** Danny Kaye
1921 W.A. Boucher	Sgt. Kouma, Sgt. Rodriguez,	**1985** Lee A. Iacocca
1922 Harold Landreth	Lt. Hudner, Capt. Millet	**1986** Erma Bombeck
1923 H.L. Gianetti	Maj. Sitter	**1987** Pele
	1953 Richard M. Nixon	

139

6 · MEN AND WOMEN IN WHITE

Over 800 volunteers make the Tournament of Roses happen every year. They work tirelessly, shepherding floats, hosting dignitaries, directing traffic, marshaling marching bands, scouting for equestrians, scooting about on red Hondas on parade day, answering questions like, "Where did I park my car?" and "Where is the toilet?" and "Which way to the Rose Bowl?" Together, they donate some 65,000 hours every year to the Rose Parade and the Granddaddy of Them All, never receiving a dime. In fact, "people from the lowest kind of occupation or the highest political office are standing guard at their barricades all night, and buying a white suit and paying for the privilege of it," marvels past President C. Lewis Edwards. And the result? Every band director, athletic director, university official, float builder, and equestrian connected to the Tournament quickly volunteers: it's the best-run festival they have ever taken part in. Bar none. But when you ask the white suiters about what they do, they modestly shrug their shoulders—"Oh, we have a lot of fun."

Enthusiastic, self-effacing, energetic, and devoted to their Tournament "jobs," the white suiters are an extraordinary group. As former Tournament manager Bill Lawson was fond of saying, he could pick up the phone, call up one white suiter, say he needed 20 people at the corner of Orange Grove and Colorado at nine o'clock the next morning, and have 30 volunteers show up. Every year the Association admits only a third of the people who apply for membership. What other volunteer group has to turn helpers away? Or what other charitable organization has to force its members to retire at age 65? The only tangible benefit of membership is the opportunity to buy tickets to the Rose Bowl (*pay* for them, mind you; white suiters only get one or two gratis). The rest is work, work, work, for a series of committees up a corporate ladder as sophisticated as that of any Fortune 500 company. But before ascending the ranks to the ruling junta of the Executive Committee, the new member must buy his white suit.

The tradition of wearing white on the First goes back to 1932 when, as past President Lay Leishman recalls, "the Tournament members were out there working the parade in their old clothes because they had been up all night. We could not find our membership when we needed them . . . So we came up with the scheme that if you wore a Palm Beach suit on New Year's Day, you had to be crazy." Today the hard-working "crazies" wear white shoes, white shirts, white socks, white skirts or pants for the women, white suits with white buttons and for a splash of color, red ties. You cannot miss them. In fact, the Tournament is said to

be the biggest customer for white suits in the nation, after the Mormon Church. The one unofficial accessory is long underwear, also white. 1986 President Fred Johnson once tried wearing his red skiing underwear, only to discover, "They gave me cream of tomato legs."

MEN AND WOMEN AT WORK

For their first few years in the Tournament, members are assigned to menial tasks. They spend New Year's Eve at lonely barricades, checking for resident or guest passes of cars entering and exiting the pre-parade route, telling the drivers, "easy right," "easy left," "easy on the brakes," or "easy on the clutch." They hang "No Parking" signs on trees and discourage parade viewers from waving "Hi Des Moines!" and "Happy New Year Duluth!" signs in front of the TV cameras. One of the most frustrating jobs 20 white suiters had one year was holding a canvas tarp over hundreds of helium balloons for a balloon release that NBC was filming. Of course, balloons kept slipping out, like popcorn from a popper, and the diligent white suiters kept stuffing them back under, to no avail. Don Fedde, who was in charge, says members still come up to him, asking, "Do you remember when . . . ?" How could he forget?

One of the least glamorous tasks would seem to be guarding the floats in the post-parade area for the two days after the parade (like celebrating Christmas on the 26th, or going to a New Year's party on the 2nd). But no job is beneath a white suiter. They enthusiastically point out the sweet rice, wild rice, and dry rice on the side of a float or describe the animation, recreating the spectacle of the day before. Besides protecting the floats, they also protect the crowds. When 1987 President Fred Soldwedel was "doing post-parade" one year, a truck parked near the barricade lost its brakes and started to roll towards the float. After getting all the spectators out of harm's way, Soldwedel thought, "Now I know why I'm here."

In his day, Lay Leishman put in an intriguing stint on the Censors Committee. The committee, which no longer exists, was set up in the '30s after a Hollywood studio entered a float with "a lot of pretty girls in real lacy costumes" on it. The outfits were modest enough—until it rained and the fabric concealed as much as a bathing suit in the *Sports Illustrated* swimsuit issue. "We had objections from the WCTU and the churches. So they appointed Max Turner and me to the Censors Committee, and if girls

145

weren't properly dressed then we took them off the float. I've been kidded since then that it was like putting a fox in with the chickens, but it wasn't that bad."

Back then the Association was all male but since 1974 it has accepted women. There are still few women in the top brass because it takes so long to move up the ladder (it took my dad 35 years to become President). The first few years bring modest demands on most members' time. But the higher one ascends, the more one is expected to do. One past president, a dentist, jokes that he only netted $6 the year of his presidency. Fred Johnson estimated that when he was president he spent about 35 percent of his work time on Tournament business. Members are lawyers, doctors, bankers, stockbrokers, salesmen, restaurateurs, owners of small businesses, and executives in large corporations. And because of the democratic nature of the organization (a meritocracy if there ever was one), it's not unusual to see an employer working for his employee or direct competitors cooperating on the same committee.

The committees vary from Community Relations and Communication to the more mundane-sounding Food Services and Properties. One ad hoc group performs the complicated task of laying out the parade—actually moving 8-by-10 inch renderings of the floats and pictures of the equestrians and bands around on a table, making sure that themes and sponsors are mixed up, not one bank's float after another or one foreign band behind another. Others chaperone the queen and court, or chauffeur the judges, or arrange to serve lunch to 4,500 tired members of 22 marching bands after the parade. Some committees require professional assistance, such as certified mechanics to help Float Construction check out the floats; while others make experts out of amateurs, teaching white suiters on Equestrian the names of horses, or those on Music the difference between a Sousaphone and a tuba.

Although a lot of jokes pass between members (the head of Equestrian is invariably presented a ceremonial pooper-scooper), they all perform their jobs with the dedication of Secret Servicemen and the earnestness of seminarians. "The quality of people is exceptional," says one member. "There's not a one I wouldn't have in my home." Another remarks, "In March I think I'm not going to do it, but in December the adrenaline starts going and I'm pressing my white suit and brushing up my white bucks." "After the war, when I came home I joined," says a third. "It's just what you do in Pasadena." Father is followed by son who

Top: Public Relations Committee puts press bleachers into place.
Left: Post Parade Committeeperson helps float rider down after parade.
Above: Linda Rillorta describes one of the floats which are on display for three days after the parade.

is followed by son who is followed by daughter, for generations. There have been over a half-dozen President fathers whose sons have achieved the same honor. None has been more influential than 1939 President Lay Leishman and his father William, 1920-21.

THE BOWL IS BUILT

"My father was a native of New Haven, Connecticut," Lay recalled in a long interview with the Pasadena Oral History Project, "and he thought there was nothing as great as something that came from Connecticut. As a child, I went back with him to New Haven and saw the Yale Bowl, and I believe he got a set of the plans which he brought back to Myron Hunt, who was a famous Pasadena architect." That year, 1921, "they took a committee down to the east bank of the Arroyo and Mr. Myron Hunt took a piece of what was then called Upson board. It was 4 feet by 8 feet and he cut a hole in the middle of it and held that out over the edge of the Arroyo Seco, and when you looked down, you could see this hole in the middle. That's where the Bowl was going to be."

The challenge was to raise the money. "Dad organized this group that sold tickets for a ten-year plan. For one hundred dollars you got a seat in the Rose Bowl every year for ten years. They sold these seats, and enough of them to raise $250,000 and the Rose Bowl was built within a year. It had somewhere around 55,000 seats. It had an open south end and a fence of wood across there. The first game, in 1923, the crowd outside the Bowl pushed the fence down and took over the seats. So five years later they closed in the south end which increased the capacity to 76,000." By then, too, the money that had been borrowed to build the Bowl was completely paid off, a laudable record in today's era of huge deficits on costly new stadiums.

The Bowl gradually expanded up to its current 100,000 capacity, as Lay continued on—like his father, serving the Tournament. After acting as President in 1939, he was chairman of the Rose Bowl Committee for the next 40 years and helped establish the Pac-10/Big Ten Pact as it stands today. He also found the Tournament its permanent home in 1959.

"Charlie Summerville, who was the locker room boy at Annandale Country Club for fifty years was a friend of mine. I was walking into Annandale to play golf one day, and he said, 'Lay, isn't it too bad what's going to happen to the Wrigley house.

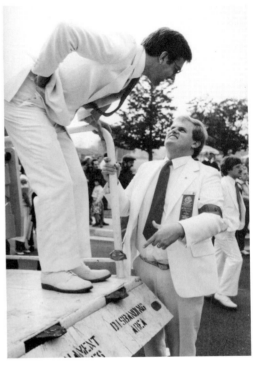

They're going to sell it.' I said, 'Oh gee, Charlie, they ought to give that to the Tournament of Roses.' He said, 'Why don't you ask for it?'" The next day when the manager of the Wrigley family's Southern California property showed up at the club, Charlie introduced him to Lay. Lay asked for the house, the manager thought it was a great idea, the Tournament hurriedly drew up papers to get tax-exempt status, and within a week, the Tournament was officially offered its distinguished new headquarters, where it's been ever since.

ON THE ROAD

The President, though, spends little time at home during the year leading up to his parade. He's constantly on the road, meeting float sponsors, college football representatives, civic

Jon Pawley, in spite of the fact that his name was sometimes misspelled, was chairman of the Formation Area Committee and was in charge of the all-important command trailer, from which parade route information is constantly coming in and going out.

groups, marching bands, his name appearing on Hilton and Holiday Inn marquees from Portland to Saint Petersburg. In the old days, when as one float sponsor says, "you could push a wheelbarrow down Colorado Boulevard and be in the parade," the President went far and wide looking for possible entrants. Back in 1955, John Biggar Sr. was pleased to come back from a trip to Alaska with a promised float from a mysterious Alaskan organization. Only later did he discover that the "bigwig" he had signed up was a sous chef at a lumber camp. Now most of the trips are made to visit well-canvassed, well-known sponsors and groups—Eastman Kodak in Rochester, Rand McNally in Chicago, FTD in Detroit—often just to say "thanks for the business." And as the Tournament's "business" has become more international, the President has increased his mileage to cover Puerto Rico, Singapore, Malaysia, Japan, Jordan, and China. 1987 President Fred Soldwedel recalled at one point that he and his wife had only spent nine nights out of 101 at home.

Despite all the international travel, some of the most exciting visits are stateside calls on high school marching bands. For the President, who may only be a modest businessman at home, it can be a rare, heady dose of the red carpet treatment. When 1986 President Fred Johnson stepped off the plane in Pensacola, Florida, girls gave his wife bouquets, the mayor of the city made an 8-minute speech, and on the tarmac the Tate High School Band launched into a rousing rendition of the "South Rampart Street Blues." It's like being royalty or the real President and First Lady. The adulation made my mother feel like Nancy Reagan, especially after receiving fan letters from band members. "I get scared every time I think about California," wrote one. "I realized you were probably just as nervous when you came to visit us. Your attitude impressed me so much that I realized I can be considerate to others even when I am nervous . . . I am enclosing my senior picture so you will remember who I am."

Everywhere they go, Presidents leave rose stickers as their unique calling card on nametags, lapels, bathroom mirrors, and windows. When the Football Committee visited President Nixon in the early '70s, even the portrait of Conrad Hilton in their hotel was wearing a rose upon their departure. Perhaps it's still there. Fred Soldwedel gave metallic cloissone roses to every band member he spoke to. "They would form long lines that took me 45 minutes to go through. The adults with them all wanted to tell you about some connection they had with the Tournament. 'My brother-in-law's cousin worked on one of the floats' they would say, or 'my sister had a neighbor who was a princess.'" And naturally, someone knew someone who was a white suiter.

This camaraderie is the very genius of the Tournament white suiters. The dentist who stays up all night directing traffic, the retired engineer who builds a special box to hold the Rose Queen's tiara, the advertising executive who vacuums the corner of Colorado and Orange Grove on January 1, the auto mechanic who spreads straw in front of the horses before they march so they will relieve themselves, the college fundraiser who dines with football heroes—the Tournament of Roses is truly theirs. They each try to bring something special to their tasks, whether it's multi-colored bouquets for the Rose Court (instead of just red), a new breed in the line-up of horses, or a new dish for the New Year's Day breakfast. "It's a chance to do something artistic," one volunteer explains. Inevitably, the sum is greater than the parts. Nevertheless one can often hear the volunteers say, "*Our* parade went pretty well this year" or "*Our* game came off better than I expected" or "*Our* floats were better than ever."

You cannot argue with them.

PART
2

THE
GAME

7 · GRANDDADDY OF THEM ALL

The Granddaddy of Them All, the oldest of the bowl games, started out as an East-West college football game which the Tournament hoped would attract more national attention to their annual pageant. For several decades, without any other bowls competing for teams, the Rose Bowl had a wide choice of schools from the East to pick. Harvard, Tulane, Brown, Penn State, Georgia, Georgia Tech, Southern Methodist, and Nebraska all made one-time appearances in the Bowl. Tennessee and Duke played twice. Pittsburgh came out four times; Alabama played six games, winning four, tying one, and losing one. Stanford and USC dominated in the West each representing the Pacific Coast Conference in eight Rose Bowls before the current Pac 10/Big Ten pact was established in 1947.

In chronicling those first few decades I have singled out players and coaches in a succeeding section—the men who came to characterize the games they coached or played. Here are some (by no means all) of the memorable games—the upsets, the close-calls, the routs, the draws, when the Rose Bowl was just becoming the Granddaddy of Them All.

1902: A POINT-A-MINUTE

Deliberate, single-minded, hard-driving, dull-humored, Fielding H. Yost came to the University of Michigan in 1901 to coach a long series of undefeated teams. In those first five years his team lost only one game, in 1905, to the University of Chicago. They outscored their opponents 2,821 to 56. From the first practice, the players grew used to hearing Yost berate them in his high-pitched, West Virginia drawl, "You'll have to hurry up." Soon he was dubbed, "Hurry Up" Yost, a nickname that stuck.

In that first season Michigan was unscored-upon, chalking up 501 points in ten games, earning their nickname, the "point-a-minute" Wolverines. The star halfback of the team, Willie Heston, was so strong that once when an opponent stood between him and the goal line, he picked up the stunned safetyman in his right hand (the ball was in his left) and ran 15 yards to make a touchdown. Yost himself was so enthusiastic about football that he once kicked a hole in a stranger's suitcase in a railroad station trying to demonstrate the proper way to kick a field goal.

Yost came to Michigan from the West Coast. The previous year he had coached at Stanford, where he was not made head coach because he was not a Stanford graduate. Whether he nursed a grudge or not, Yost relished the opportunity to meet his

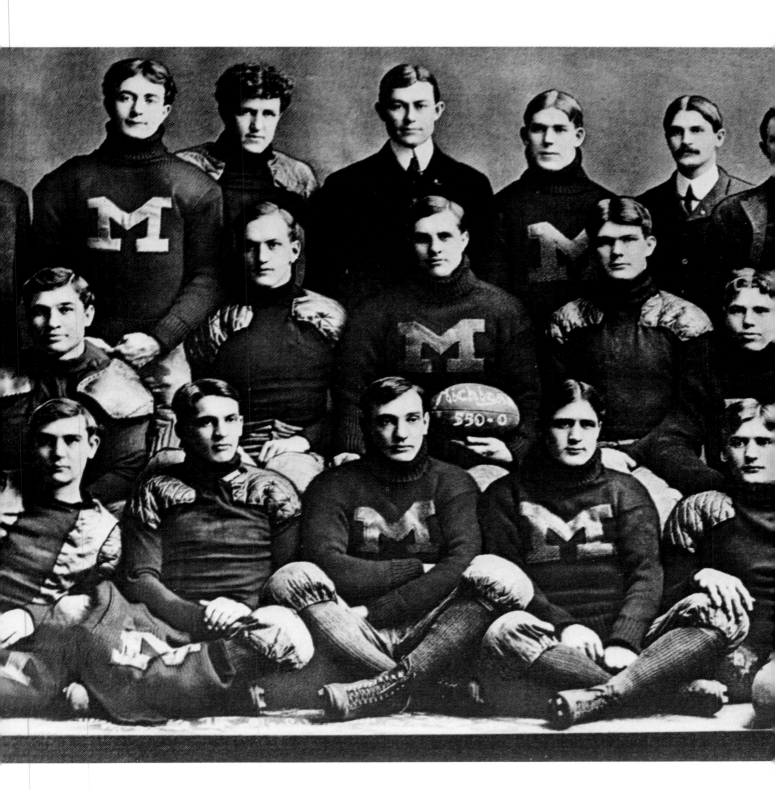

First Tournament East-West Football Game Jan. 1, 1902 - Michigan vs Stanford

Above: Some 8,000 fans jammed Tournament Park, projected to hold only 1,000. Tallyhos, farm wagons, cars, and feet were the modes of transportation.
Opposite: The game turned into a rout, as undefeated Michigan humbled Stanford, the West Coast representative, 49-0.

former team in Pasadena with his unbeatable "point-a-minute" squad.

It was a rout. Stanford lost 49-0. They were outblocked, outrun, outtackled, outkicked, and outcoached. In those days football was more violent, played without thick pads, hard helmets, or the forward pass. The Michigan team, sporting "calves like piano legs and arms to match," as a local paper put it, wreaked havoc on the Stanford team. Stanford guard William Roosevelt, a second cousin of President Teddy Roosevelt, played a quarter of the game with his right leg broken and two fractured left ribs. He stuck it out, like a good Roosevelt should. Another teammate limped off the field, "no longer able to move his stiffening body because the ligaments of his right shoulder had been torn asunder."

Amidst the carnage, Michigan fullback Neil Snow rushed five touchdowns—a Bowl record that still stands. Kicker Ev Sweeley—who punted nearly 900 yards that day, averaging almost 40 yards a kick—also made four field goals. In an era when field goals were worth five points, those kicks counted for a lot.

With eight minutes left in the game, Stanford had had enough. The Stanford captain approached the Michigan captain and said, "If you are willing, we are ready to quit . . ." As dusk began to fall, so ended the first Tournament of Roses football game.

Although it was not followed by another football game for 14 years—partly because no other Western team was willing to face such humiliation—that first Rose Bowl established some important precedents. It was a huge draw. The Tournament had anticipated a crowd of only a thousand, but when over 8,000 pushed their way into the stands in Tournament Park, they knew they had a success. Typically enough too, it began and ended in a huge traffic jam, with tallyhos, farm wagons, and autos crowding the road. But most importantly it showed that the center of collegiate football was moving westward. Yost was the first to challenge Eastern dominance in college football. His "point-a-minute" team tallied up scores that attracted the attention of the Ivy League. And he ended that first year not by going east to play the traditionally dominant Princeton or Yale, but by going west to show his stuff in California.

However inauspicious for California teams or unbalanced a contest for the spectators, it was the start of a glorious cross-country rivalry.

1922: ALL THE PRESIDENTS MEN

After the rout of 1902, the Tournament returned to their previous format of staging sporting events in Tournament Park after the parade. There were exciting chariot races inspired by the novel *Ben Hur*. There were auto races and ostrich races and even an exotic race between an elephant and a camel (the elephant won). But considering the enormous expense of mounting and training a team of chariot horses, and after a few nearly disastrous

accidents, it seemed best to go back to football. In 1916, Brown lost to Washington State, 14-0, on a wet, cold January 1 before a disappointing crowd of 7,000 spectators (they had had 25,000 the year before). The Tournament lost money on that event, but they decided nonetheless to stick to football, inviting such national champs as Penn and Harvard to compete with the best from the West. Gradually the crowds increased so that by 1922, 40,000 fans crowded into the rickety stands at Tournament Park. On a damp January 2 (New Year's Day that year was a Sunday), Washington and Jefferson, 14-point underdogs, confronted an undefeated University of California team.

This was Cal's second consecutive appearance in the Bowl. The previous year they had destroyed Ohio State, 28-0, a loss so humiliating that the Big Ten did not come back to the Bowl for 25 years. California's "Wonder Teams" (as they were called) did not lose a single game between 1920 and 1924. Their undisputed star in the '21 Rose Bowl was end Brick Muller. In that game Brick threw a pass that has been variously reported as traveling anywhere from 50 to 70 yards on the fly. Cocky, probably overconfident in 1922, Cal was the defending champ. And they were playing virtual unknowns.

"All I know about Washington and Jefferson is that they're both dead," quipped a California sportswriter at the announcement that W&J would play. This small Pennsylvania college with fewer than 500 students seemed an unlikely choice to represent the East in the Bowl. But they had gone undefeated that year, beating powerhouses like Syracuse, Pittsburgh, and Carnegie Tech. Nicknamed "the Presidents," Washington and Jefferson brought only 16 men to Pasadena, and played the entire game with just eleven. They held Cal to only two first downs in the game, both in the first half. Cal was able to gain just 49 yards all day, and most amazingly, considering the arm of Brick Muller, they never completed a pass.

Washington and Jefferson refused to be intimidated. The Presidents ignored Brick Muller's 60-yard warm-up passes on the sidelines. While journalists were calling them derogatory names, like "Willie and Jake," predicting a scathing loss, the Washington and Jefferson team pooled their money and bet on themselves. When the invincible Brick Muller made his first appearance in the second quarter, W&J captain Russ Stein put out his muddy hand, saying, "I'd like to shake hands with the great Brick Muller." Then he looked down at his dirty hand and wiped it on Brick's clean jersey. By the time the rest of the W&J team had followed suit,

Muller was infuriated, humiliated, and filthy.

Even so, Washington and Jefferson never scored a point. They came close on a 35-yard touchdown run, but offsides was called against tackle Stein and they never had a scoring opportunity again. Cal almost scored in the fourth quarter; however, Muller's pass to halfback Crip Toomey was dropped under the force of a W&J tackle, and Cal's "Wonder Team" stumbled off the field with no points.

A scoreless tie seems like nothing to cheer about, but for that feisty team from a small Pennsylvania college it was an undisputed victory.

1925: AN ALL-STAR CAST

After seeing 40,000 people crowd into the flimsy Tournament Park stands (on a rainy day, no less), the Tournament knew better accommodations had to be built. In 1923, the fruit of their efforts was used for the first time. Modeled after the legendary Yale Bowl in New Haven, the new stadium was originally a horseshoe holding 57,000 spectators. Enclosed five years later, it took on the bowl shape it has today. It was named "the Rose Bowl" almost by accident by a Pasadena sportswriter, Harlan "Dusty" Hall, doing part-time public relations work for the Tournament. The name stuck and the New Year's Day tradition got its enduring surname.

Opposite: Cal's superstar, Brick Muller. Because of assorted injuries, Muller couldn't play until the second quarter. Below: Gutsy W&J, with only 16 players, made no substitutions and held Cal to a scoreless tie.

In 1925, the Rose Bowl hosted an all-star cast when Notre Dame came out to California for its first and only Bowl appearance. They played against Stanford, coached by the brilliant tactician Glenn "Pop" Warner. Warner was an innovative genius who did more than any other coach to make college football a mental contest rather than a game of brute strength. A great offensive tactician, he introduced imaginative plays involving fakes, reverses, hidden balls, and unbalanced lines. In the Bowl that year he used a double wingback formation—a formation that allowed a wide variety of plays—almost exclusively. Stanford was receptive to his "thinking man's" football.

Notre Dame was coached by the legendary Knute Rockne. Magnetic, charismatic, and eloquent, Rockne almost single-handedly built the Notre Dame football dynasty that exists today. He could be cynical with his teams, remarking when things were going poorly, "Remember girls, let's not have any rough stuff out there." And then in turn he could give one of his "Win one for the Gipper" half-time tearjerker speeches. He took an intense interest

in his players' personal lives, coaching them through romantic problems, academic troubles, domestic crises, but above all he hoped to instill them with his redemptory belief in football. "Football," he once said, "teaches a boy responsibility as a representative of his college, responsibility to his teammates, responsibility in controlling his passions. . . . Football brings out the best there is in everyone."

The stars of the Notre Dame team were the four men in the backfield, christened by sportswriter Grantland Rice "The Four Horsemen," an alias that immortalized them nationwide. They were halfback Don Miller, fullback Elmer Layden, halfback Jim Crowley, and quarterback Harry Stuhldreher, and they performed as a tightly-knit unit, never losing a game their senior year. Supporting them were seven equally strong linesmen, dubbed the "Seven Mules."

Making their way slowly westward, the Notre Dame team stopped for a week in Tucson, Arizona, where Knute Rockne told them to be careful about reaching in their pockets for a handkerchief, lest a lawless bandit think they were drawing their guns. Earlier he had been irked when Stanford's president expressed reluctance to let the Indians meet the Irish in the Bowl because of Notre Dame's supposed academic inferiority to Stanford. Rockne was soothed only when a Rose Bowl publicist planted a news story talking about the rigorous law studies of the Four Horsemen.

The Stanford player that most intimidated Notre Dame was fullback Ernie Nevers, one of the finest players Stanford has ever had. Broad-shouldered and square-chinned like a caricature of a football player, Nevers was a powerhouse runner, an aggressive tackler, and punted for a 42-yard average. When he saw the famous publicity shot showing the Four Horsemen in their helmets astride four horses, he said, "I'd like to play those guys someday," adding with understatement, "with or without the horses."

He almost missed his chance. Nevers broke one ankle early in the '24 season and fractured his other ankle towards the end. He had to sit out the Cal-Stanford game at season's end, and the casts were taken off his ankles only ten days before the Rose Bowl. On January 1 when Coach Warner told him to suit up, he exclaimed, "How can I play? I can hardly walk." "Don't worry," Pop said, "I've built you some braces. You're going to be just fine." In his garage, Warner had fashioned some braces out of an inner tube and aluminum. Ernie put them on and still could not walk.

"You're still my starting fullback," Warner affirmed, "You might not be able to play more than 10 minutes, but go out and try."

Rockne started out the game with his usual ploy, putting in his "shock troops" of second stringers for a few minutes so the Four Horsemen and Seven Mules could observe the action. When they entered the game it proved a tougher contest than they were used to. On amazing, sustained drives, Stanford would approach the goal line and then get intercepted. Nevers ran, passed, and kicked, doing everything possible to get his team into the end zone. As Rockne later said, "He ripped our line to shreds. He skirted the ends. He forward-passed, and he kicked." When one excited Notre Dame sophomore entered the game during the height of battle, the team looked to him for advice. Stammering, he said, "Fellas, R-R-Rock s-s-says the-the trouble is y-you're not s-s-stop-ping N-N-Nevers!"

On one controversial play Nevers appeared to get the ball in the end zone. One referee raised his hands and the Stanford fans rose to their feet. But then it was judged to be just a few inches short. Nevers, with his ankles taped so tightly that his blood could hardly circulate, ended up playing all 60 minutes of the game. Stanford lost, 27-10, but Nevers' statistics were astounding. In fact, he actually rushed for more yards than the Four Horsemen put together; fumbles and interceptions cost Stanford the game.

Rockne was as gracious in victory as Warner was in defeat, but Nevers was the one who earned a standing ovation at the end of the game.

1934: THE VOW BOYS VS. THE UNDERDOGS

If Stanford often complained that they did not play their academic equals in the Pacific Coast Conference, they got their chance in 1934. That year they faced Columbia University in the Bowl. You could find as many aspiring lawyers, doctors, dentists, and engineers on the Columbia team as on Stanford's, but that was where comparisons stopped. These were Stanford's "Vow Boys." As freshmen they had "vowed" to beat their conference rivals, USC, and they did three years in a row. Three consecutive times they came to Pasadena. Five of them became All-American, including tackle Bob "Horse" Reynolds, the only football player to have played every minute in three consecutive Rose Bowls. In this era of platooning offensive and defensive players, it's a record likely to stand.

Opposite: Coach Lou Little led Columbia to a 7-0 victory over Stanford, although the Indians helped with eight fumbles.
Above: Quarterback Cliff Montgomery (33) directed the fake that sprung Al Barabas (far right) for the game's only touchdown.
Left: Vike Francis scores Nebraska's first TD in a losing cause against Clark Shaughnessy's Stanford team and the T-formation.

And Columbia? They were smaller (averaging 17 pounds lighter per man), slower, less powerful, and the perpetual underdogs of the Ivy League—a match for a good high school team at best.

When Columbia received the Rose Bowl invitation, they were enthusiastic, if not awed. The New York press, on the other hand, could only foresee disaster. As John Kieran wrote in the *New York Times*, "Please keep the East safe hid/From famine and from slaughter and from Bowl of Roses bid!" When that bid was accepted, he continued in an elegiac vein, *"Moriturus te saluto!* For Columbia I roar! And tell them to remember me but please forget the score!"

Like Notre Dame before them, Columbia took their time to get to the West. Coach Lou Little worried that the balmy Southern California weather would sap his boys' strength so he kept them practicing at high school fields across the country. At several stops along the way they polished and honed a single mysterious play: KF 79.

Little's worries about weather were misplaced. Instead of basking in the sun, California was buried in rain and mud on January 1. Twelve inches of rain fell on Pasadena in the 48 hours before the game. On game morning the field was so wet the Fire Department had to drain it with hoses and pumps. Bands rode in buses and pretty girls on floats wore some of the first clear plastic raincoats (one of my mother's earliest memories of the Rose Parade). Only 35,000 fans showed up for the match, less than half the usual crowd.

Stanford was confident of victory even in the miserable weather. After all, they were a three- or four-touchdown favorite. But Columbia was not intimidated. Even before the game Columbia fullback Al Barabas told an interviewer, "The seat of a big guy's britches can get just as hot as a little fellow's, if you sit down on them often enough."

Barabas, it turned out, would score the game's only touchdown. In the second quarter, on Stanford's 17-yard line, Columbia's quarterback called for KF 79, their secret weapon. This play was little more than a hidden-ball trick, with an unbalanced line to throw off the Stanford defense. The quarterback took the ball from the center and handed it quickly to Barabas who ran swiftly around the unguarded left side. At the same time, the quarterback pretended to hand it off to the right halfback who plowed into the line. When Columbia's quarterback, Cliff Montgomery, looked up and saw the Stanford team totally baffled, he knew it had worked. Undetected until it was too late, Al Barabas sprinted to the goal line.

The game did not end there. The Stanford Cardinals came back and made a big push in the third quarter, getting down to the three-yard line. Four times they tried to get the ball across; four times they failed. On the fourth down Barabas saved the day by recovering Stanford's fumble. "Barabas he was a robber," newsmen wrote, quoting the Bible.

Years later when the Columbia team held a reunion and watched Couch Lou Little's films of the game, they could see how agonizingly close they came to losing. Watching each play, watching Stanford advance slowly only to be thwarted again and again, Al Barabas finally cried out, "Turn it off, Lou. I'm still afraid they might score!"

Of course, they never did. Columbia beat Stanford, 7-0.

1941: THE T-FORMATION

The "Vow Boys" had two more tries in the Bowl before they finally won, defeating SMU, 7-0. For the rest of the decade Stanford dropped back down to the bottom of the Pacific Coast Conference. But when they returned to the top it was in a moment of glory and dazzling innovation.

In 1940, Stanford got a new coach, Clark Shaughnessy, and with him a new formation. Obsessive, eccentric, Shaughnessy lived, ate, drank, and breathed football. He was constantly diagramming new plays, scribbling on napkins, file cards, blackboards and folders. A policeman once pulled him off the road for what looked like drunken driving. It was not. Shaughnessy, a strict teetotaler, had been diagramming a new play on a foggy windshield and, abstracted in thought, he paid little attention to the road. He would even devise plays as he watched the team from the sidelines. He would hand a 5" by 7" file card to his Stanford quarterback, who would read it to the team in the huddle and execute it on the field.

What he brought the Stanford team was the revolutionary T-formation. Up until then the dominant offense in college football had been the single wing, where the objective was to spread your opponent's defense as thin as possible and run through the holes. But with the T-formation the strategy changed so that the offense would bring the defense in tight and then run around it or throw over it. The biggest change was in appearance. Instead of standing a few yards back from the center, the quarterback stood right

167

behind him, actually touching him, to receive the snap. Suddenly the quarterback had a whole new set of options—to pass, lateral back, hand off, fake, or run. And because the ball came to the quarterback right between the center's legs, it was harder for the defense to follow.

In Stanford's Frankie Albert, Coach Shaughnessy found the perfect quarterback to help introduce the T. Not too fast, not a strong blocker, Albert was not an impressive tailback on the single-wing. But he was brilliant as a quarterback on the T, where he was required to pass, fake, and engage in a lot of sleight-of-hand. An irreverent, intuitive player, he was the only one on the team audacious enough to tease Shaughnessy. Every once in a while he would feign injury, briefly torturing his none-too-amused coach. But on the field it was the same talent for deception that made Albert a star. He would stand outside the huddle as though he were wondering what to do, then call a play as though he had improvised it. Taking the ball from the center, he could baffle his opponents who were unaccustomed to the new T. He was even the first to "bootleg" the ball—faking the defense as though he were going to pass, only to keep the ball and run.

Stanford plowed over its opponents in the 1940 season. They came to the '41 Bowl undefeated. There they met Nebraska in its only Rose Bowl appearance. Both teams wore red and white, confusing the fans. When Nebraska made its first touchdown in the first quarter, many Stanford fans rose to their feet to cheer for the Indians. Frankie Albert strolled over to his solemn coach and said with his characteristic confidence, "Don't worry, Coach, we haven't had the ball yet."

When they got the ball they tied the score, only to have Nebraska come back with another touchdown (although no extra point) in the second quarter. Then just before the half Frankie Albert made an impressive 40-yard touchdown pass and kicked for the extra point. That put Stanford ahead, 14-13. In the third quarter, halfback Pete Kmetovik made an exciting 38-yard punt return touchdown run that featured some sensational blocking by the Stanford team. Even 175-pound Frankie Albert knocked his man down—twice, actually. As he later explained, they kept bumping into each other trying to follow Kmetovik's unpredictable path. Albert made the kick for the extra point, his third of the day, and it was a victory for Stanford and one for the T.

1942: A GAME AWAY FROM HOME

In 1942, the Rose Bowl almost did not happen. On December 7, 1941, the Japanese bombed Pearl Harbor and a week later the general in charge of the armed forces in the eight Western states cancelled the game. Such a large gathering was considered too great a security risk. No amount of arguing by the Tournament or the teams that were invited could change his mind. He was adamant. There would be no game in the Bowl.

Through some hurried telephone work by the Pacific Coast representative, Oregon State, the game was moved to Durham, North Carolina, home of the Eastern representative, Duke University. This would be Duke coach Wallace Wade's sixth Rose Bowl game. His first had been back in 1916 when he played guard for Brown University. Then in 1926, '27, and '31, he had brought outstanding teams from Alabama to the Bowl, one of which featured star halfback Johnny Mack Brown, who stayed on in California to become a Hollywood cowboy. "We were nothing but little country boys when we started," Brown once said. "Then Coach Wallace Wade made something out of us." The last time Wade had been in the Bowl he was coaching Duke in 1939, when they lost under the last-minute onslaught of USC's Doyle Nave's passing. On that occasion, Wade refused to congratulate Nave or shake hands with USC's coach Howard Jones. He also made some tactless remarks to the press about Southern California. Happy to appease his West Coast detractors, Wade agreed to host the only Rose Bowl game played outside of Pasadena.

LON STINER
COACH
OREGON STATE

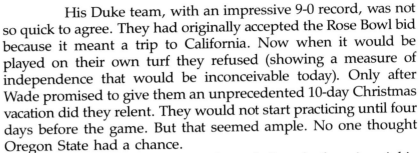

His Duke team, with an impressive 9-0 record, was not so quick to agree. They had originally accepted the Rose Bowl bid because it meant a trip to California. Now when it would be played on their own turf they refused (showing a measure of independence that would be inconceivable today). Only after Wade promised to give them an unprecedented 10-day Christmas vacation did they relent. They would not start practicing until four days before the game. But that seemed ample. No one thought Oregon State had a chance.

Oregon State coach Lon Stiner believed otherwise. A big bruiser of a man weighing 230 pounds, he worked his team rigorously to meet their first Rose Bowl challenge. Not above dramatizing his pep talks, once, before a game, he went charging towards the locker-room door. After ramming himself against a locked door, he charged again, ripping it off its hinges. The message was clear. In Durham before the game, he staged a mock fight with the policeman leading the motorcade into the stadium. At a prearranged moment he yelled and screamed at the patrol man, who hollered back for the benefit of the players in the bus. When Stiner was done, the Oregon State team members were ready to kill.

Duke was in for a surprise. Through some textbook passing and running, Oregon State held them at the third quarter, 14-14. Then came a spectacular pass play when Oregon State's Bob Dethman threw a long bomb to Gene Gray. It went 70 yards and for years was the longest pass in Rose Bowl history. It gave Oregon State a touchdown and the edge that helped them win the game. Duke came close when blocking back Tommy Prothro (future coach of Oregon State and UCLA) passed into the Oregon State end zone. The ball was intercepted, and then the Oregon State player who caught it was tackled, giving Duke a safety. That fourth-quarter play turned out to be a blessing in disguise for Oregon State because it gave them a chance to kick out of their territory, and it stalled Duke at their own goal for the rest of the game. Oregon won, 20-16.

Wallace Wade was much more gracious this time in defeat. He congratulated the winning team, spoke highly of them to the press, and in his most generous move, he offered to pay the Tournament of Roses Association's costs out of Duke's "Rose Bowl" revenue. Because the game had not actually been played in the Bowl, the Tournament was deprived of their usual cut of the gate. They had no money to cover their expenses, including the manager's salary. Records show they accepted Wade's offer.

ROSE BOWL SCORES (through 1946)

1902 Michigan (10-0) Fielding "Hurry Up" Yost **49**
Stanford (3-1-2) Charles M. Fickert **0**

1916 Washington State (6-0) W.H. Dietz............ **14**
Brown (5-3-1) E.N. Robinson................ **0**

1917 Oregon (6-0-1) Hugo Bezdek **14**
Pennsylvania (7-2-1) Robert Folwell **0**

1918 Mare Island (5-0) Hugo Bezdek.............. **19**
Camp Lewis (5-1-1) W.L. Stanton............. **7**

1919 Great Lakes (6-0-2) C.J. McReavy **17**
Mare Island (10-0) W.H. Dietz................ **0**

1920 Harvard (7-0-1) Robert Fisher................ **7**
Oregon (5-1) Shy Huntington **6**

1921 California (8-0) Andy Smith.................. **28**
Ohio State (7-0) J.W. Wilce **0**

1922 California (8-0) Andy Smith.................. **0**
Washington & Jefferson (10-0) Earle Neale..... **0**

1923 USC (7-1) Elmer Henderson.................. **14**
Penn State (6-3-1) Hugo Bezdek **3**

1924 Washington (10-1) Enoch Bagshaw **14**
Navy (5-1-2) Robert Folwell **14**

1925 Notre Dame (9-0) Knute Rockne.............. **27**
Stanford (7-0-1) Glenn "Pop" Warner **10**

1926 Alabama (9-0) Wallace Wade **20**
Washington (10-0-1) Enoch Bagshaw.......... **19**

1927 Stanford (10-0) Glenn "Pop" Warner.......... **7**
Alabama (9-0) Wallace Wade **7**

1928 Stanford (7-2-1) Glenn "Pop" Warner **7**
Pittsburgh (8-0-1) John Sutherland **6**

1929 Georgia Tech (9-0) William Alexander **8**
California (7-1-1) C.M. "Nibs" Price **7**

1930 USC (9-2) Howard Jones **47**
Pittsburgh (9-0) John Sutherland **14**

1931 Alabama (9-0) Wallace Wade **24**
Washington State (9-0) Orin "Babe"
Hollingbery **0**

1932 USC (9-1) Howard Jones **21**
Tulane (11-0) Bernie Bierman **12**

1933 USC (9-0) Howard Jones **35**
Pittsburgh (8-0-2) John Sutherland **0**

1934 Columbia (7-1) Lou Little **7**
Stanford (8-1-1) Claude "Tiny" Thornhill....... **0**

1935 Alabama (9-0) Frank Thomas................. **29**
Stanford (9-0-1) Claude "Tiny" Thornhill....... **13**

1936 Stanford (7-1) Claude "Tiny" Thornhill **7**
SMU (12-0) Madison Bell **0**

1937 Pittsburgh (7-1-1) John Sutherland **21**
Washington (7-1-1) James Phelan.............. **0**

1938 California (6-4) Leonard Allison **13**
Alabama (8-0-1) Frank Thomas................ **0**

1939 USC (8-2) Howard Jones **7**
Duke (9-0) Wallace Wade..................... **3**

1940 USC (7-0-2) Howard Jones **14**
Tennessee (10-0) Robert Neyland **0**

1941 Stanford (9-0) Clark Shaughnessy **21**
Nebraska (8-1) L.M. Jones.................... **13**

1942 Oregon State (7-2) Alonzo Stiner **20**
Duke (9-0) Wallace Wade..................... **16**

1943 Georgia (10-1) Wally Butts **9**
UCLA (7-2) Edwin C. Horrell................. **0**

1944 USC (7-2) Jeff Cravath **29**
Washington (4-0) Ralph Welch **0**

1945 USC (7-0-2) Jeff Cravath **25**
Tennessee (7-0-1) J.H. Barnhill............... **0**

1946 Alabama (9-0) Frank Thomas................. **34**
USC (7-3) Jeff Cravath **14**

8 · THE PLAYERS AND COACHES OF THE GAME

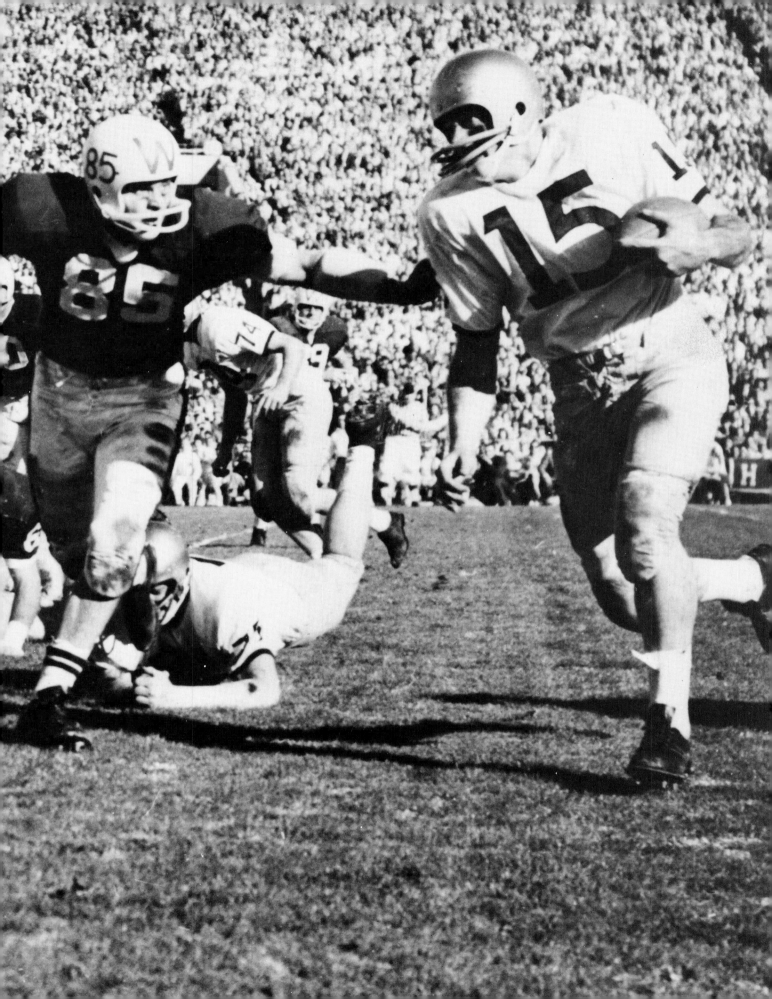

Jim Hardy, USC's captain and quarterback when they defeated Tennessee, 25-0, in the '45 Rose Bowl, called his own number at the end of the game so he could keep the football as a trophy. Once he was tackled, he got up and ran for the locker room with his prize. John Robinson, USC's coach in the '77, '79, and '80 Bowls, remembers playing for Oregon in the Oregon-Ohio State game in 1958 when Oregon lost, 10-7. He went in for the last seven seconds and when the gun went off, a Buckeye lineman grabbed the ball, saying, "That's all, kid." In the 1965 game, Michigan's Mel Anthony ran 84 yards for a touchdown, a record that still stands. Moments later, someone let a pig loose on the field to ridicule Anthony's record run, until several fans tackled it.

Heisman Trophy winners have put in some of the most disappointing performances of their careers in the Bowl. Second-string freshmen have appeared out of nowhere to challenge long-standing records. Winning coaches have lost miserably one year, only to come back and win the next. Players and coaches, winners and losers, have given the Bowl excitement, pathos, surprises, and thrills year after year. Some are officially recognized with the Player of the Game award after the game. Others walk back to the bus in silence. Here are a memorable few who coached, played, won, or lost in the Bowl.

1921, 1922: BRICK MULLER

The first college player from the West to be voted All-American, Cal end Brick Muller was big, fast, and powerful. 6' 2" tall and weighing 190 pounds, he not only played football, but in the spring he was one of the University of California's top track stars. In his event, the high jump, he was so good he earned a silver medal at the 1920 Olympics. In football he could run, pass, and catch like no other player of his day. During his four years at Berkeley he never played a losing game—and that includes two Rose Bowls.

Brick's greatest moment in the Bowl came over a much-disputed pass in 1921 when Cal was playing Ohio State. In the second quarter Cal was ahead, 7-0, when between plays Cal fullback Archie Nesbit pretended to be injured. He lay on the ground at the center of a carefully rehearsed line of scrimmage, with Brick moving nonchalantly to an unexpected backfield position. Suddenly, at a prearranged signal, the "injured" fullback jumped to his feet and hiked the ball before Ohio State could rush

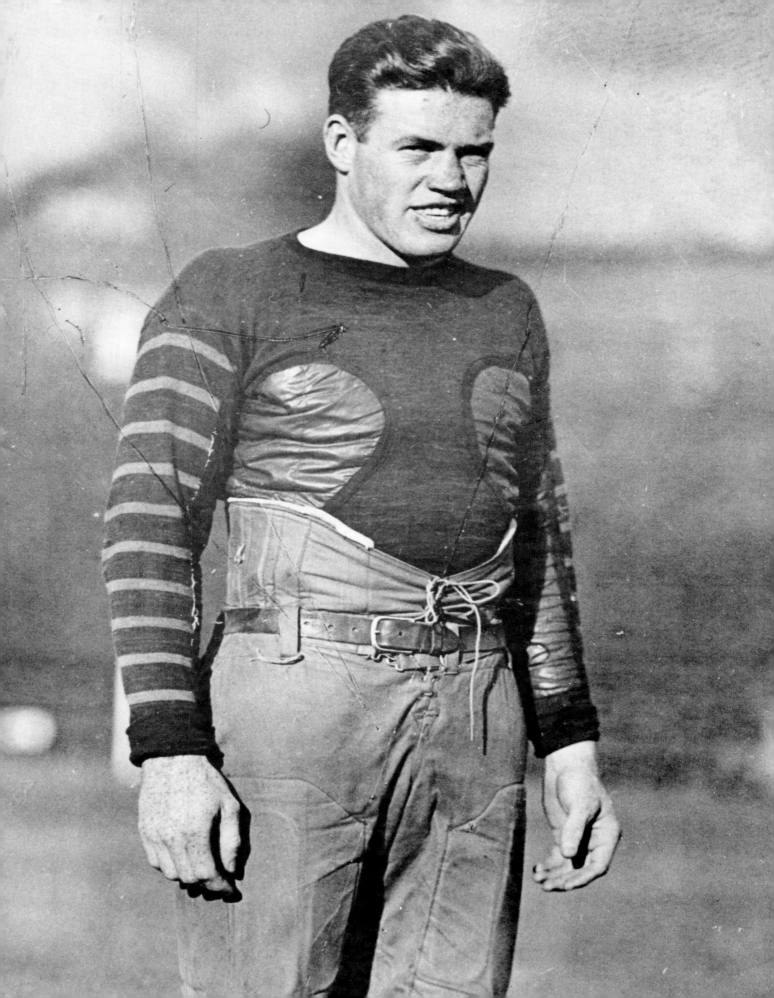

Above: Roy Riegels takes off on his historic "wrong-way" run.
Opposite: Riegels after the run. The play occurred during the 1929 California–Georgia Tech game, and proved decisive in the Tech victory. Although remembered mostly for the run, Riegels was an All-Coast center and captain of his team.

Muller. As the Cal end Brodie Stephens ran long down the field, Muller was lateraled the ball on his own team's 47-yard line. Just when Stephens reached the goal line, Muller threw a low pass right into his arms and the Bears scored a touchdown.

The dispute came when writers and officials tried to measure the distance the ball had traveled. On the ground, California had gained 53 yards (and a TD), but Muller threw the ball on a diagonal, lengthwise, across the field for 60, 62, who knows, maybe 70 yards. At a time when a football was shaped more like a loaf of bread than an aerodynamically designed spheroid, it was an amazing feat, bringing Brick Muller well-deserved fame as not only the best in the West, but also one of the top passers in college football.

1929: ROY RIEGELS

Roy Riegels's notoriety, on the other hand, is of a more dubious sort. For years his feat in the 1929 game haunted him. He would go to a restaurant or a hotel and some astute waiter or desk clerk would say, "Aren't you the one . . .?" Or after he thought the events of that game had long been forgotten, someone would make an egregious error in some other game, and suddenly his name would come up. "That reminds me of Wrong-Way Riegels."

Roy Riegels came to Pasadena his junior year when his team, the University of California, played Georgia Tech. He was a highly esteemed center, voted All-Coast for the second year in a row and elected to serve as team captain the following season. He was average size for a lineman then, 170 pounds, and a fast runner—a little too fast as it turned out.

It was 0-0 in the second period and Georgia Tech had the ball deep in their own territory. On a running play Stumpy Thomason, the Georgia ball carrier, was tackled so hard he fumbled the ball somewhere near the Tech 34. It bounced once, then Riegels picked it up and began to run (in those days you could run with a fumble). First he veered towards the nearby Tech goal line, and then he shifted and ran the wrong way, heading straight for his own goal 65 yards away. For a brief moment (before he realized what he had done), it must have been thrilling. Half the stands were yelling at him, no opponent was near him and a heroic touchdown seemed to be within reach. With all the noise, he could not hear his teammate Benny Lom running after him, shouting, "Stop, you're going the wrong way!" It was not until Riegels reached the one-yard line that Lom managed to tackle him. On the next play, a punt, the California kicker bobbled the snap and Georgia Tech pounced on the loose ball in the end zone and scored a safety, two points. Those two points proved to be the margin of victory when the game ended, 8-7, Tech.

Many explanations were made for Riegels's error. He was dizzy; he had been hit in the head; he had been turned around by one of his opponents; he became confused swerving out of the way of several tacklers. Riegels himself never tried to make any excuses for himself. He played honorably in the second half of the game—which included a bizarre moment when Benny Lom attempted a quick kick and the ball deflated! And in his last year at Cal he captained a team that lost only one game. Over the years he grew philosophic about his error, saying, "It's just one of those things you have to accept." But probably the wryest assessment of Riegels's run came from coaching great Alonzo Stagg. "What did you expect?" said Stagg. "After all, football centers are always looking at the world upside down."

1935: HOWELL AND HUTSON

Millard "Dixie" Howell, a triple-threater from Alabama, could kick, run, and pass superbly. In the '35 Rose Bowl he was chiefly praised for his arm, becoming "the human howitzer from Hartford, Alabama," in sportswriter Grantland Rice's immortal words. There his best passes went to end Don Hutson, making them an inseparable team.

The balls flew "like arrows from Robin Hood's trusting bow," according to one sportswriter. They dropped into Hutson's waiting hands "like an apple from a tree," according to another Alabama player and future coach, the legendary Bear Bryant. Hutson could catch running, diving, jumping, leaping, forwards, backwards, in the air, on the ground. In one game he caught a ball after pivoting full speed around a goalpost, leaving his defender tackling air. He was so fast that one spring day when he was playing baseball for Alabama, he wore his running shorts under

FOOTBALL EXTRA

4141 HERALD Express **NIGHT FINAL**

ALABAMA BEATS STANFORD. 29-13

Santa Anita Results

Santa Barbara Float Wins in Rose Parade

his uniform. During an appropriate lull, he stripped into his track togs, ran over to a meet on an adjacent field, clocked a 9.8 hundred-yard dash, and then returned to the baseball game.

"I couldn't recognize Hutson if I met him face to face," said the captain of the Stanford team after the 1935 Bowl game. "I spent all afternoon chasing him. The rear view, I will never forget." Hutson caught six passes, amassing 164 yards for the Alabama team, a reception record unbroken until 1985. Halfback Howell completed nine of twelve passes and made a thrilling 67-yard touchdown run, casually waving at the Stanford team as he passed them.

After the Bowl, Don Hutson went on to an impressive career in pro football, where he became the Alabama Antelope, catching so many passes that he established an NFL record as the highest-scoring receiver, with 99 touchdowns. An innovator as well, he was the first player to put black shoe polish on his cheekbones to cut out the sun's glare and the first receiver to run pass patterns.

In the years since Howell and Hutson played in the Bowl, passing has become much more common in college football. Then it was an aerodynamic display, as one newspaperman said, "the like of which has never been seen in football on the Coast."

1939: HOWARD JONES AND DOYLE NAVE

No college coach has a Rose Bowl record to equal USC's Howard Jones. John McKay also brought the Trojans to the Bowl often enough to win five times, but he lost a few, too. Howard Jones never lost a Rose Bowl. Under his expert guidance USC triumphed in 1930, '32, '33, '39, and '40. There were close calls, such as the victory over Duke in '39 (7-3), and routs, such as USC's two thrashings of Pittsburgh in '30 and '33 (47-14 and 35-0, respectively).

Jones and his younger brother Tad grew up in Ohio and went on to Exeter and Yale, where they both played football, neither of them ever participating in a losing game. Howard stayed on at Yale where he was the first paid football coach at the University. Tad later served as Yale's head coach, where he made the legendary, hyperbolic pregame speech, "Gentlemen, you are about to play football for Yale against Harvard. Never in your lives will you do anything so important again."

If possible, Howard was more serious and certainly more humorless than his brother. He never drank, he avoided reporters

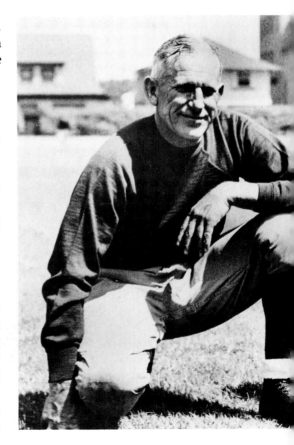

Opposite: Little-used, fourth-string quarterback Doyle Nave led USC to a thrilling last-minute comeback against Duke in the 1939 game.
Below: Howard Jones, humorless and conservative, nevertheless coached USC into five Bowl games—and won every one of them.

assiduously, he intimidated his players with his stern demeanor, and he coached a conservative game that stressed running and blocking and was short on razzle-dazzle. At times, if USC was too far ahead, he would ask the quarterback to hold back, lest they score too many points and be overconfident for the next week's game. But Howard Jones also had a thoughtful and sensitive side. After USC trounced Notre Dame in 1931—the first time the two teams had played since Rockne's death—Jones did not attend the victory celebration, asking instead for directions to Rock's gravesite. There he led the Trojans in a short memorial service.

Ironically, Jones's most memorable game in the Bowl had less to do with his fine coaching than with a bit of last-minute heroics from a fourth-string sub. It was 1939 and USC was facing a strong squad from Duke University. In the fourth quarter, with less than three minutes to go, Duke was clinging to a slim 3-0 lead. USC's assistant coaches, calling plays from the Rose Bowl press box, had already given up and were moving down to the field. That's when a lone junior coach manning the phone took things into his own hands. Impetuously, he rang up Jones and told him, "Send in Doyle Nave and have him throw passes to Krueger."

Doyle Nave was a fourth-string quarterback. He had only played 28 and a half minutes that whole season. Evidently, in his time off the field he had practiced some tight passing patterns with his fellow sub, end "Antelope Al" Krueger. When Nave entered the game, USC was on Duke's 34-yard line. In a spectacular execution of the two-minute drill, he marched USC into the end zone, and to a thrilling victory, 7-3.

Later in the locker room, Doyle Nave said, "I wonder if I'll get a letter now."

"Son," someone responded, "you're going to get the whole alphabet."

1960, 1961: BOB SCHLOREDT

Only two players have ever been named the Player of the Game in the Rose Bowl two years in a row, and one of them was Bob Schloredt. Quarterback for the Washington Huskies in 1960 and 1961, he led his team to victory both years, ending thirteen years of dominance by the Big Ten.

That first year, Washington met Wisconsin, a seven-point favorite in the Bowl. The Huskies had not been to Pasadena since 1944, and although they had done well in the regular season, ending up 9-1, no one expected them to wallop Wisconsin, a bigger team with a higher national ranking.

In the first quarter the Huskies started out with a 48-yard play-by-play drive down the field that culminated in a touchdown. Minutes later, the other co-Player of that Game, Husky George Fleming, kicked a 44-yard field goal—a record that stood until 1985. Still in the first quarter, Fleming ran 53 yards on a punt return for a touchdown, and by the end of the first 15 minutes of play Washington had a sizable lead, 17-0.

Wisconsin never caught up. A daring quarterback, Schloredt went for the yardage on fourth down. He passed when he had to, or carried the ball boldly over the line, or faked handoffs and snuck up the middle. In 1960's Bowl game, Schloredt rushed for 81 yards and completed four of seven passes for 102 yards. He was an All-American quarterback that year and the previously unheralded Huskies were suddenly the unbeatable Purple Gang. Their conquest of Wisconsin, 44-8, represented the widest margin of victory for a Pac-10 team over a Big Ten team until it was matched in 1985.

At the start of the 1961 season, Schloredt, with his picture on the cover of *Sports Illustrated*, looked like a promising candidate for the Heisman Trophy. Unfortunately, he broke his left collarbone in mid-season and was out of action for several weeks. In the meantime Washington squeaked by three of its A.A.W.U. competitors (or Athletic Association of Western Universities, as the Pac-10 was then known) by only one point and landed in the Bowl ranked sixth nationally. This time they had to face the nation's number one team, Minnesota, a big, powerful, heavyweight team with an aggressive defensive front line made up of players like 243-pound guard Tom Brown. To get around them Washington had to depend on speed and finesse.

This time it took a long first half for Washington to build a lead, 17-0. But once again Schloredt confounded his opponents with the same deft ball-handling, including a quarterback sneak from the Minnesota one-yard line. He averaged 12 yards a carry on ground plays and 41 yards on seven punts. In the second half, Washington preserved their lead by playing more conservatively—relying on their defense—and won, 17-7. This time Schloredt did not share the award for Player of the Game; he won it on his own.

The most startling thing about Bob Schloredt was that he was practically blind in one eye. At the age of five he had been playing with firecrackers, dropping them in Coke bottles, when

Right: Washington
quarterback Bob Schloredt.
Schloredt is one of only two
players to win the Rose Bowl
Player of the Game two
years in a row. Amazingly,
Schloredt was 95 percent
blind in one eye.
Opposite: 1969 opponents
and 1968 teammates both
hug O. J. Simpson. During
his two years at USC,
Simpson won Player of the
Game and the Heisman
Trophy.

one exploded and hit him in the left eye. Scar tissue formed over it and he lost all but about five percent of its vision. From childhood on he grew used to operating with what would be a debilitating handicap for most quarterbacks. "I learned to judge distance by the size of the person, but don't ask me how I did it . . . The fact that it happened so early allowed me to compensate."

And compensate he did.

1968, 1969: O. J. SIMPSON

The first time O.J. came to the Bowl he was only watching. It was 1967 and he had just transferred to USC from junior college. He saw his new team lose to Purdue, 14-13, and standing in the locker room afterwards he consoled his teammates, "Don't worry about it. We'll be back next year." They were, that year and the next.

O.J.'s story is a rags-to-riches tale. Raised in a poor, pre-dominantly black San Francisco neighborhood, he grew up among gangs and high school dropouts in an area of government housing projects. Early on, O.J. showed enormous promise as an athlete, but his high school grades were not good enough to get him into a big football university. He entered San Francisco City College, and while there, ran for 26 touchdowns in two years, averaging 9.9 yards a carry.

Heavily recruited, he chose USC. There, under the coaching of John McKay, he polished the tricks that would make him the Trojans' star tailback the next two years. A sprinter capable of a 9.4 hundred-yard dash, O.J. also ran on the USC track team, participating on the 440-yard relay team that set the world record in 1967.

O.J. lived up to his promise—and then some. In his two years of playing Pac-10 ball, he amassed nearly 3,500 yards rushing and scored 36 touchdowns. He was elusive, fast, strong, and a quick thinker, delighting fans with his fancy footwork. In one of

USC's most exciting games ever, he led the Trojans to the 21-20 victory over UCLA that would bring them to the 1968 Rose Bowl. When he met UCLA quarterback Gary Beban in the locker room afterwards, he said, "It's too bad one of us had to lose." Only O.J. could say something like that and sound like he meant it.

In the '68 Rose Bowl, the number-one Trojans faced Indiana. O.J. carried the ball 25 times for 128 yards and scored the team's two touchdowns, giving USC a solid win, and earning for himself laurels as Player of the Game. In 1969 USC faced Ohio State in a tough contest between the number one and number two nationally ranked teams. Both were undefeated, both were con-

ference champions, both coached by legends—McKay and Woody Hayes. Without a doubt the most thrilling play of the game was O.J.'s 80-yard, first-quarter touchdown run (four yards short of Mel Anthony's record TD run in 1965). But USC was hampered by two costly interceptions and three fumbles (two of them Simpson's). Ohio State won, 27-16, in the first of 14 consecutive Bowl games featuring either Ohio State or Michigan from the Big Ten (or "Big Two-Little Eight" as journalists started calling them). O.J. had the consolation of the Heisman Trophy he had won that year—and two matchless years of carrying the ball for Troy.

Against Ohio State in the 1971 Rose Bowl, Stanford quarterback Jim Plunkett continually found holes in the Buckeye defense. Plunkett, the Heisman winner, led the underdog Indians to a 27-17 victory over an Ohio State team that had lost once in three years.

Ohio State coach Woody Hayes exhorts his troops. He modeled himself after George Patton, and was one of the worst losers in the history of football. In eight trips to the Rose Bowl, Hayes's teams won four and lost four.

1971: JIM PLUNKETT

Like O.J.'s, Jim Plunkett's story is another Cinderella tale. He grew up in humble circumstances in San Jose, the third child of a sightless Mexican couple (with enough German-Irish ancestry to own the un-Mexican-sounding last name of Plunkett). His mother was totally blind. His father was legally blind, so that he could only read by holding a newspaper inches away from his face, and he had problems counting out change at the newsstand he ran. At an early age, Jim became very independent by necessity, working at odd jobs, shying away from organized school social events, immersing himself in athletics instead. He pitched on the baseball team, wrestled in the winter, and was quarterback on a football team that garnered two league championships. With a wide choice of colleges, he chose nearby Stanford so that he would not be far from his parents.

The first few years at Stanford were not easy. A shy, introspective young man, Plunkett did not fit in easily in the high-spirited, gregarious campus life. Most weekends he went home to be with his family. Furthermore, his success as a football player was not assured. Several weeks before his freshman year, he was operated on for a tumor on his neck. It turned out to be benign, but the operation slowed him down his first season. The next year Coach John Ralston wanted to make him a defensive end on varsity. Plunkett held out for quarterback. Ralston finally acceded by red-shirting him that year—he would be active in practice but benched during games—assuring him of three full seasons on varsity starting in 1968. (According to NCAA rules no one could play college varsity for more than three years.)

In those three years, Plunkett displayed his talent as a passer, leading the Stanford Indians to 22 wins, 8 losses, and 2 ties. He threw bombs with amazing accuracy—one went for 96 yards. In three seasons he completed 530 out of 962 passes for a total of 7,544 yards and 52 touchdowns. In the spring of 1970 he was eligible to be drafted by the NFL but he stayed behind one more semester to graduate—and to take Stanford to the Rose Bowl. When asked which he would prefer, the Heisman Trophy or an invitation to the Bowl, Plunkett did not hesitate. "The Rose Bowl . . . because I can do that with my team."

He did it with his team, but he was the deciding factor. Against an Ohio State team that had only lost once in three years, Stanford was touted as a 10-point loser. To win they took to the air, playing a passing game against the Buckeyes' strong ground

game. Again and again Plunkett discovered holes in the Ohio defense and hit one of his receivers. In one catch, tight end Bob Moore leaped up between two defenders and caught the ball on the four-yard line to set up a touchdown. The final touchdown that clinched the game came on another Plunkett pass, this time to flanker Randy "the Rabbit" Vataha. Stanford won, 27-17, and Jim Plunkett claimed not only the Heisman Trophy but also a Rose Bowl victory. He admitted, "I can't remember a more jubilant time in my life."

WOODY

Woody Hayes did not get off to the best start when he brought Ohio State out to Pasadena for the first time. It had rained all that New Year's Day in 1955, so by the time the game started, the field was ankle-deep in mud. Woody took one look at the field and suggested that the bands from the two schools cancel their halftime shows to save what little grass was left. "I think bands are a fine thing, but they owe their popularity to football, not the other way around." After his team's 20-7 win over USC, Woody ingratiated himself further to West Coast fans by stating, "My coaches who sat in the press box said we would have beaten USC by a higher score on a dry field . . . There are about four, possibly five, teams in the Big Ten that could beat USC . . . Big Ten teams are better in the Rose Bowl because they are raised on tougher competition."

Was there ever a man so brash, so temperamental, so tactless, or so rude? Probably not on the sidelines of the Rose Bowl. Just to watch him during a game was to witness a display of emotion worthy of a temperamental opera diva. He would bite his fist, throw down his cap and jump on it, bully a player or heckle a referee. When he lost, he locked himself in the dressing room and refused to talk to reporters, sometimes for hours. Even his wife admitted, "I don't get upset when I am at a game and some fan yells at Woody and calls him an SOB. Why should I? I've called him that myself."

What finally made Woody so likable, or at least forgivable, was that he clearly cared so much about his team, about college football, and about the Rose Bowl. A devoted student of military history, Woody saw each game as another battle, a Marne or a Guadalcanal, in the history of college football. General George S. Patton was a hero of his and he never failed to be impressed that Patton had once ridden and hunted in the Arroyo

Seco where the Bowl now stood. "What better place to win a game than where the greatest tank commander of all time was born," he once said. In 1961 when he learned that the Ohio State faculty had voted against the Buckeyes' going to Pasadena that January (for fear of overemphasis of athletics), he was outraged. When he heard that members of his team had quelled the near-riot on campus that followed, he beamed with pride.

Woody's efforts at public relations were generally dismal. In 1969 he showed up a half hour late for the Kickoff Luncheon, and then the program had to be rearranged so that he could fit another quick afternoon practice in for his boys. While in Pasadena, he often cut out all their extracurricular fun—the Beef Bowl, the trip to Disneyland, the tour of Hollywood studios—to get his boys in shape. When asked what he feared most about USC, he grunted, "Not a damn thing!" This was, after all, the self described "old-cuss," who at the pre-Bowl big dinner said, "We don't buy football players at Ohio State. We sell 'em on a Christmas vacation in California each year."

Woody's relations with the press sank to their lowest in 1973 when a Los Angeles *Times* photographer accused Hayes of ramming his camera into his face about five minutes before the start of the game, allegedly saying, "that'll take care of you, you SOB." The photographer only dropped a criminal battery charge after Hayes sent an appropriate letter several weeks later. The following year, when Woody returned to Pasadena, he was all charms and smiles, refusing to discuss any past unpleasantness, even allowing his team to be interviewed and photographed. "You've treated me damn great," said the New Reformed Woody. "And I've treated you fellas a helluva lot better. You see? It's a two-way street."

For years, Woody was accused of bringing an unimaginative ground game to Pasadena, and getting beaten in the air by some fine Pac-10 passing. In fact, he once said, "When you throw a forward pass, there are only three things that can happen, and two of them are bad." But when he won in 1974, it was through a good deal of passing—129 yards to be precise. He was a good winner too, talking animatedly to the press. But as a loser, well, in his own words, "Show me a good loser . . . and I'll show you a loser."

In eight trips to the Rose Bowl, Woody won four and lost four, but those four losses all came in the 1970s and stand out above the victories, especially the final one, a humiliating 23-10 defeat to 14th-ranked UCLA. There was Woody crossing the field

193

Above: Anthony Davis (28) breaks through the Ohio State line, pursued by Randy Gradishar (53), during USC's 1973 Rose Bowl triumph. Opposite top: Woody Hayes in a lighter moment. Opposite bottom: John McKay with 1974 Queen Miranda Barone. McKay took his team to the Rose Bowl so many times (eight), he became as much of a fixture as the queens themselves.

even before the game had ended to grudgingly congratulate UCLA coach Dick Vermeil. "Congratulations . . . but they [our team] screwed up." And Woody refused to talk to anyone—even his own players—afterwards. And Woody sitting in glum silence on a dark bus parked in the Arroyo, amidst the red flares and nighttime fog and traffic jam of his last Rose Bowl game.

THE SILVER FOX

The University of Southern California showed up so often at the Bowl in the 60s and 70s that even Californians (especially UCLA fans) found it tiresome. When Ronald Reagan was speaking at the 1975 Kickoff Luncheon, he remarked, "The thing that impresses me about the Tournament of Roses is how everything is exactly the same year after year. The magnificent parade, the brilliant floats, the pageantry, Woody Hayes, John McKay. . . ." He pointed out that Coach McKay did not even have to be shown where to sit; he was merely told, "Just go to your usual place."

Still, it was hard to resent a repeat visit from John McKay. He was polite, eloquent, grateful to be there, and a guarantee of fine football on New Year's Day. No other coach has been to the Rose Bowl as many times as McKay, and only one other coach (Howard Jones from USC) has won as often. McKay's Trojans lost three games—in '67, '69, and '74—and won five— in '63, '68, '70, '73, and '75. Win or lose, McKay always retained his affability. Even archrival Woody said somewhat wistfully, "There are coaches who can be nice and win, guys like John McKay. Me, I can't be nice and win. It's not my way."

McKay, unlike Woody, always kept the event in perspective. "The best thing about it," he once remarked, "is that it eliminates New Year's Eve. You don't have to be up screaming and yelling at midnight. This way, nobody complains if you get into bed at 8:30." He was occasionally willing to use only 12 of the allotted 16 days of practice, explaining, "I feel the Rose Bowl should be a reward, not a punishment." And even if he lost, you never heard him complaining.

His complaints after the game tended to be about the national polls, either that they were too quick to name a winner or that they were too slow—especially if USC were the obvious choice. In 1973, after the Trojans' 42-17 victory over Ohio State, McKay asked cynically, "Is there anyone else Associated Press wants us to play before we get the national title?"

Several of McKay's games in the Bowl were really close calls—one of the reasons, the white-haired coach claimed, that he was no longer a red-head. Often, though, McKay could be blamed for making a tense game tenser. For instance, he could never accept a tied game in the Bowl. "Gentlemen," he would say, "We didn't come here to play for a tie." In 1967, when the Trojans scored in the last two minutes to make it 14-13, with Purdue still in the lead, McKay went for the two-point conversion rather than kick for a tie. Purdue blocked the pass and USC lost. But when history repeated itself in 1975, with the score 17-16 after a Trojan touchdown that narrowed Ohio State's lead, USC made a successful two-point conversion and won the game 18-17.

McKay could be flippant when he was displeased with his team for playing poorly. "I could make those impassioned pep talks," he once explained to the press, "but I figure it's better to keep the kids loose. I don't want to be responsible for any suicides." Usually, though, he was quick to give credit where it was due. When Sam "Bam" Cunningham surprised everyone by scoring four touchdowns in the 1973 game against Ohio State, McKay said, "I owe Sam something. He was a great runner but I made him a blocker for three years. He's the best runner I ever ruined."

It seems fitting that the last Rose Bowl game of McKay's career was the one in which his son John made the last-minute winning touchdown. It was a thrilling moment for USC and presented a grand opportunity for McKay to indulge in some well-justified, paternal pride. But McKay, as always, kept the moment in cool perspective. "Are you proud of your son?" he was asked. "Yes," he replied, "I'm very proud. I'm proud of *both* my daughters and *both* my sons."

1977, 1979, 1980: CHARLES WHITE

USC's Heisman Trophy winner Charles White came after the McKay dynasty, but he followed in another great Trojan tradition that O.J. Simpson was quick to recognize, that of the great USC runners. "Me, Anthony Davis, Ricky Bell," O.J. told writer Joe Jares, "I think Charles may erase all our names . . . He has great explosion, he *sees* everything. He's a darter, he's not a power runner or anything, but he has that explosion into the hole and that's what you've got to have. . . . " White made his auspicious Rose Bowl debut in 1977 (against Michigan) replacing USC's star tailback Ricky Bell, who was helped off the field after his fourth carry of the day with a case of whiplash that resulted in a mild brain concussion. Buoyed by chants of "Do it for Ricky," freshman Charles White rushed for a total of 122 yards in the game, only 33

yards less than the Michigan team's ground yardage. He sacrificed himself in the second quarter, leaping over the line of scrimmage after taking a fake handoff from quarterback Vince Evans, giving Evans an easy score; and in the fourth quarter White made the winning touchdown on a seven-yard run. Admitting afterwards that he was at first a little scared about having to go in for the great Ricky Bell in the all-important Rose Bowl, White said the feeling did not last long. "After I got hit, I settled down."

By the time Charles White returned to the Bowl the second time, in 1979, he was an acknowledged star. Although he struggled to make 99 yards in the game, his career total equaled 4,195 yards, the highest in the Pac-10, and he was only a junior. Fortunately he would have another chance in the Bowl, because his achievement in Pasadena that year, when USC faced Michigan again, is still shrouded in controversy. It centers around a phantom touchdown in the second quarter . . . or was it a touchdown?

White had the ball as he dove over Michigan's left guard and headed for the end zone, but then he dropped it. The ball bounced on the one-yard line and Michigan recovered. The Michigan players swore he had not crossed the goal line before fumbling, but the line judge—ironically enough a Big Ten official— signalled a TD, giving Southern California a 14-3 lead. No matter how many times the instant replay showed White without the ball as he crossed the goal line, the umpire's call could not be revoked. As White said, shrugging, "It's over now, it's history." History gave USC another win over Michigan, 17-10 and White the honor of Player of the Game, shared with Michigan quarterback Rick Leach.

White's final Rose Bowl appearance was in an exciting, down-to-the-wire match between two top-rated college teams with perfect seasons: number one Ohio State vs. USC, number two or three depending on which poll you read. White played the game with a stomach flu and a nose held together with tape; still he ran for 247 yards on 39 carries, both current Rose Bowl records. With the help of a tight offensive line, including 6'7" 280-pound guard Anthony Munoz, White was able to carry the ball on long sustained drives. Once, White rushed up the middle for 45 yards, only to fumble when he neared the goal line. But any errors White might have made were wiped out when he led USC in a dramatic, fourth quarter drive for 83 yards. White himself carried for 71 of those yards, and of course, he dove into the end zone for the winning touchdown. By the time Ohio State got the ball back, there was only a minute and a half left in the game, and USC

won, 17-16.

In his four years at USC Charles White had learned how to be modest. He chose to give credit to his offensive linemen and USC. "That's our style, our game. We wear people down." The well-earned accolade had to come from Coach Robinson, who simply said, "Charlie White is the greatest player I have ever seen."

BO

For one of the winningest coaches of all time, Bo Schembechler has had the worst luck in the Rose Bowl. In 1970, the first year he brought his Michigan team out to Pasadena (after his first season as Michigan's head coach), Bo did not make the game. He was confined to St. Luke's Hospital with a mild heart attack. He was helpless. He could not do anything but watch TV as his team lost, 10-3, to USC. It was Michigan's first defeat in five Rose Bowl appearances and a bad omen. "He had called every single offensive play for us all year," Jim Mandich, the U of M captain, said afterwards of his ailing coach. "I'm sure his loss handicapped us." For a team that had averaged 420 yards per game during the year, the absence of the coach undoubtedly hurt. In the Bowl that year, the team gained only 289 yards on offense and they could not even score a touchdown.

Bo returned two years later, bringing a team with a perfect season (during which they scored an amazing 421 points). They faced an unpredictable 16th-rated Stanford squad. That December was a wet one in Southern California and Bo's pre-Bowl practice sessions were continually hampered by rain and muddy fields. When the team hit the dry ground in the Arroyo Seco they were not at their best . . . and they lost by only one point, 13-12. Sure, Stanford had a lot of luck, but as Bo once said, "Anytime you get within a touchdown [of your opponents], you're good enough to win," and one point is close, frustratingly close.

Then there was Bo's team that he felt should have gone to the Bowl in 1974. Both Ohio State and Michigan ended the regular season that year with ten wins and one tie; Ohio state had gone to the Bowl the previous year and Bo felt it was his and Michigan's rightful turn in '74. No longer bound by a no-repeat clause, the Big Ten athletic directors voted to send what they thought was the stronger team. Ohio State went (and won) and Bo stayed home, miffed.

Michigan has had important players injured before the

game, like star running back Glenn Doughty in 1970, and injuries during the game, such as those suffered by quarterback Steve Smith and tackle Rich Strenger in 1983. There have been dubious touchdowns scored against them, such as Charles White's in 1979; and there have been dramatic, last-minute comebacks by Michigan that still did not bring them victory—they scored three touchdowns in the last 20 minutes of the 1978 game . . . and still lost. As Bo himself said, "Fate just went against us." People even began to make unkind Bo Bowl jokes, such as the one about his wife Millie saying, "I always serve my husband his breakfast cereal on a plate because if I put it in a bowl he'd probably spill it."

The thing about Bo is that no matter how it burned him up, he never pulled a Woody in Pasadena. Dutiful, hat-in-hand, he showed up at the post-game press conference and said polite things like: in '77, "I make no apologies. They [USC] are the best team I've seen this year;" or in '79, "That [USC] is the best team in the country;" or in '83, "To UCLA's credit, they never turned the ball over . . . they ran the ball pretty well on us." Was this the man who in a heated argument was supposed to have thrown a chair right back at Woody?

Sure, maybe there was a hint of the Midwestern firebrand in 1987 when Michigan lost to first-timer Arizona State University, 22-15. After the game, Bo complained about distracting crowd noise from the ASU boosters, who outnumbered the Michigan fans, 2 to 1. "You can't operate when you can't hear," he said, "I'm not making excuses; that's the way it is." He ungratefully added that it would be nice if the Big Ten teams got as many Rose Bowl tickets as the Pac-10. (Nobody bothered to remind him that that was in the contract the Big Ten had agreed to since the beginning of the pact.) But then Bo was human. He had to admit, time and again (seven times to be precise), "I'm getting tired of coming to *this* press conference. I'm tired of losing here." Then he would leave with the parting shot, "We'll keep doing it until we get it right."

Michigan did, on the sixth try, in 1981. They beat Washington soundly, 23-6. Bo smiled jubilantly and said, "I've come off that field five times with my head down. Now I'm smoking a cigar and smiling. I'm on top of the world. I feel great about everything." After such a moment it's easy to see why former USC coach John Robinson would say about Bo, "I'd love to have a son play for him. He'd come out of there a much better person." Honest, forthright, fiery when pushed, Bo is a man who never, ever, gives up . . . at least when it comes to the Rose Bowl.

Michigan coach Bo Schembechler, of whom USC coach John Robinson said, "I'd love to have a son play for him. He'd come out of there a much better person." Schembechler lost his first five tries at the Rose Bowl, but in 1981 his Wolverine team finally bested Washington, 23-6.

201

ROSE BOWL PLAYER OF THE GAME

1902	Neil Snow, FB	Michigan
1916	Carl Dietz, FB	Washington State
1917	John Beckett, T.	Oregon
1918	Hollis Huntington, FB	Mare Island
1919	George Halas, E	Great Lakes
1920	Edward Casey, HB	Harvard
1921	Harold "Brick" Muller, E	California
1922	Russell Stein, T	Washington & Jefferson
1923	Leo Calland, G	USC
1924	Ira McKee, QB	Navy
1925	Elmer Layden, FB	Notre Dame
	Ernest Nevers, FB	Stanford
1926	Johnny Mack Brown, HB	Alabama
	George Wilson, HB	Washington
1927	Fred Pickhard, T	Alabama
1928	Clifford Hoffman, FB	Stanford
1929	Benjamin Lom, HB	California
1930	Russell Saunders, QB	USC
1931	John Campbell, QB	Alabama
1932	Erny Pinckert, HB	USC
1933	Homer Griffith, QB	USC
1934	Cliff Montgomery, QB	Columbia
1935	Millard "Dixie" Howell, HB	Alabama
1936	James Moscrip, E	Stanford
	Keith Topping, E	Stanford
1937	William Daddio, E	Pittsburgh
1938	Victor Bottari, HB	California
1939	Doyle Nave, QB	USC
	Al Krueger, E	USC
1940	Ambrose Schindler, QB	USC
1941	Peter Kmetovic, HB	Stanford
1942	Donald Durdan, HB	Oregon State
1943	Charles Trippi, HB	Georgia
1944	Norman Verry, G	USC
1945	James Hardy, QB	USC
1946	Harry Gilmer, HB	Alabama
1947	Claude "Buddy" Young, HB	Illinois
	Julius Rykovich, HB	Illinois
1948	Robert Chappius, HB	Michigan
1949	Frank Aschenbrenner, HB	Northwestern
1950	Fred Morrison, FB	Ohio State
1951	Donald Dufek, FB	Michigan

1952	William Tate, HB	Illinois
1953	Rudy Bukich, QB	USC
1954	Billy Wells, HB	Michigan State
1955	Dave Leggett, QB	Ohio State
1956	Walter Kowalczyk, HB	Michigan State
1957	Kenneth Ploen, QB	Iowa
1958	Jack Crabtree, QB	Oregon
1959	Bob Jeter, HB	Iowa
1960	Bob Schloredt, QB	Washington
	George Fleming, HB	Washington
1961	Bob Schloredt, QB	Washington
1962	Sandy Stephens, QB	Minnesota
1963	Pete Beathard, QB	USC
	Ron VanderKelen, QB	Wisconsin
1964	Jim Grabowski, FB	Illinois
1965	Mel Anthony, FB	Michigan
1966	Bob Stiles, DB	UCLA
1967	John Charles, DB	Purdue
1968	O.J. Simpson, HB	USC
1969	Rex Kern, QB	Ohio State
1970	Bob Chandler, FL	USC
1971	Jim Plunkett, QB	Stanford
1972	Don Bunce, QB	Stanford
1973	Sam Cunningham, FB	USC
1974	Cornelius Greene, QB	Ohio State
1975	Pat Haden, QB	USC
	John McKay, SE	USC
1976	John Sciarra, QB	UCLA
1977	Vince Evans, QB	USC
1978	Warren Moon, QB	Washington
1979	Charles White, RB	USC
	Rick Leach, QB	Michigan
1980	Charles White, RB	USC
1981	Butch Woolfolk, RB	Michigan
1982	Jacque Robinson, RB	Washington
1983	Don Rogers, FS	UCLA
	Tom Ramsey, QB	UCLA
1984	Rick Neuheisel, QB	UCLA
1985	Tim Green, QB	USC
	Jack Del Rio, OLB	USC
1986	Eric Ball, TB	UCLA
1987	Jeff Van Raaphorst, QB	Arizona State

INDIVIDUAL ROSE BOWL RECORDS (modern records are 1947 to present)

TOTAL OFFENSE
Most Plays: 57—Ron VanderKelen, Wisconsin vs. USC, 1963 (406 yards)

Most Yards Gained: 406 Ron VanderKelen, Wisconsin vs. USC, 1963 (5 rushing, 401 passing)

Highest Average Gain Per Play: 21.6—Bob Jeter, Iowa vs. California, 1959 (9 for 194)

Most Touchdowns Responsible For (TDs scored and passed for): 5—Neil Snow, Michigan vs. Stanford, 1902 (scored 5)

Modern: 4—Rick Neuheisel, UCLA vs. Illinois, 1984 (passed for 4); 4—Sam Cunningham, USC vs. Ohio State, 1973 (scored 4); 4—Pete Beathard, USC vs. Wisconsin, 1963 (passed for 4); 4—Eric Ball, UCLA vs. Iowa, 1986 (scored 4)

PASSING
Most Passes Attempted: 48—Ron VanderKelen, Wisconsin vs. USC, 1963 (completed 33)

Most Passes Completed: 33—Ron VanderKelen, Wisconsin vs. USC, 1963 (attempted 48)

Highest Percentage of Passes Completed (Min. 15 comp.): 78.9%—Charles Ortmann, Michigan vs. California, 1951 (15 of 19)

Most Passes Had Intercepted: 3—Mike Tomczak, Ohio State vs. USC, 1985 (attempted 37; 3—Jack Trudeau, Illinois vs. UCLA, 1984 (attempted 39); 3—Steve Juday, Michigan State vs. UCLA, 1966 (attempted 18); 3—Bill Siler, Washington vs. Illinois, 1964 (attempted 17); 3—Ron VanderKelen, Wisconsin vs. USC, 1963 (attempted 48); 3—Bob Celeri, California vs. Ohio State, 1950

Most Yards Gained: 401—Ron VanderKelen, Wisconsin vs. USC, 1963 (completed 33 of 48)

Most Touchdown Passes: 4—Rick Neuheisel, UCLA vs. Illinois, 1984; 4—Pete Beathard, USC vs. Wisconsin, 1963

Longest Passing Play: 76 (TD)—Rick Leach to Curt Stephenson, Michigan vs. Washington, 1978

RECEIVING
Most Passes Caught: 11—Pat Richter, Wisconsin vs. USC, 1963 (163 yards); 11—Ronnie Harmon, Iowa vs. UCLA, 1986 (102 yards)

Most Yards Gained: 172—Cris Carter, Ohio State vs. USC, 1985 (caught 9)

Most Touchdown Passes Caught: 2—Karl Dorrell, UCLA vs. Illinois, 1984 (5 receptions); 2—Wally Henry, UCLA vs. Ohio State, 1976 (5 receptions); 2—Hal Bedsole, USC vs. Wisconsin, 1963 (4 receptions); 2—George Callanan, USC vs. Washington, 1944 (4 receptions); 2—Bill Gray, USC vs. Washington, ,1944 (3 receptions); 2—Don Hutson, Alabama vs. Stanford, 1935; 2—Harry Edelson, USC vs. Pittsburgh, 1930; 2—Johnny Mack Brown, Alabama vs. Washington, 1926

KICKOFF RETURNS
Most Kickoff Returns: 5—Ralph Clayton, Michigan vs. Washington, 1978 (102 yards); 5—Allen Carter, USC vs. Ohio State, 1974 (101 yards); 5—Kevin Harmon, Iowa vs. UCLA, 1986 (90 yards)

Most Yards on Kickoff Returns: 178—Al Hoisch, UCLA vs. Illinois, 1947 (4 returns)

Highest Average Gain Per Return: 44.5—Al Hoisch, UCLA vs. Illinois, 1947 (4 for 178)

Longest Kickoff Return: 102 (TD)—Al Hoisch, UCLA vs. Illinois, 1947

INTERCEPTIONS
Most Passes Intercepted: 3—Bill Paulman, Stanford vs. SMU, 1936; 3—Shy Huntington, Oregon vs. Pennsylvania, 1917

Modern: 2—Tommy Haynes, USC vs. Ohio State, 1985 (8 yards); 2—Don Rogers, UCLA vs. Illinois, 1984 (44 yards); 2—Bob Stiles, UCLA vs. Michigan State, 1966 (42 yards); 2—George Donnelly, Illinois vs. Washington, 1964 (30 yards); 2—Joe Cannavino, Ohio State vs. Oregon, 1958 (5 yards); 2—Matsock, Michigan State vs. UCLA, 1954 (67 yards); 2—Stan Wallace, Illinois vs. Stanford, 1952 (54 yards); 2—PeeWee Day, Northwestern vs. California, 1949; 2—Tom Worthington, Northwestern vs. California, 1949

Most Yards on Interception Returns: 148—Elmer Layden, Notre Dame vs. Stanford, 1925 (2 interceptions)

Modern: 67—John Matsock, Michigan State vs. UCLA, 1954 (2 interceptions)

Longest Interception Return: 78 (TD)—Elmer Layden, Notre Dame vs. Stanford, 1925

Modern: 68 (TD)—Russell Steger, Illinois vs. UCLA, 1947

RUSHING
Most Rushes: 39—Charles White, USC vs. Ohio State, 1980 (247 yards)

Most Yards Gained: 247—Charles White, USC vs. Ohio State, 1980 (39 rushes)

Highest Average Gain Per Rush: 21.6—Bob Jeter, Iowa vs. California, 1959 (9 for 194)

Most Touchdowns Scored by Rushing: 5—Neil Snow, Michigan vs. Stanford, 1902

Modern: 4—Sam Cunningham, USC vs. Ohio State, 1973 (2,1,1,1 yards); 4—Eric Ball, UCLA vs. Iowa, 1986 (30,40,6,32 yards)

Longest Run: 84 (TD)—Mel Anthony, Michigan Vs. Oregon State, 1965

PUNTING
Most Punts: 21—Everett Sweeley, Michigan vs. Stanford, 1902

Modern: 9—Marty King, USC vs. Michigan, 1979 (386 yards); 9—Larry Cox, UCLA vs. Michigan State, 1966 (374 yards); 9—Len Frketich, Oregon State vs. Michigan, 1965 (394 yards)

Highest Average Per Punt: 52.7—Des Koch, USC vs. Wisconsin, 1953 (adjusted to current state rules)

Longest Punt: 73—Don Bracken, Michigan vs. Washington, 1981

PUNT RETURNS
Most Punt Returns: 9—Paddy Driscoll, Great Lakes Navy vs. Mare Island Marines, 1919 (115 yards)

Modern: 6—Rick Sygar, Michigan vs. Oregon State, 1965 (50 yards)

Most Yards on Punt Returns: 122—George Fleming, Washington vs. Wisconsin, 1960 (3 returns)

Highest Average Gain Per Return (Min. 2): 40.7—George Fleming, Washington vs. Wisconsin, 1960 (3 for 122)

Longest Punt Return: 86 (TD)—Aramis Dandoy, USC vs. Ohio State, 1955

9 · HALFTIME

Preceding pages: Michigan's band goes through its paces in the seven and a half minutes allotted it. Bands have to depend on the grid of the field to orient themselves.
Above: The familiar USC Trojan.
Opposite: Arizona State, relative newcomer to the Rose Bowl, marches with the aplomb of an oldtimer. Bands that practice throughout the year in the warm weather are deemed to have an advantage.

A
t the Rose Bowl in 1981, Michigan beat the University of Washington, 23-6, a decisive victory for Coach Bo Schembechler after five humiliating Bowl losses. But when it came to the battle of the bands, Michigan's preeminence was not so clear cut. In their pre-game show, the precision-perfect Michigan band did its signature opener, a floating block letter "M" moving across the field, formed by over 200 band members marching at a fast tempo with their traditional high knee lifts. When they burst into the fight song "The Victors," the Michigan fans rose to their feet, shaking blue and gold pompoms, making their corner of the Bowl look like a field of blooming flax blowing in the wind.

Washington, on the other hand, came on at the half in a flood of purple, 160 band members joined by rally squad girls. They too formed a configuration honoring one of their state's hallowed institutions. But in the wide, shallow Bowl, this was a little hard to read at first. What was it? The Columbia, Mt. Rainier, the Seattle Space Needle? No, it was none other than Mt. St. Helens, creaking and rumbling, the Sousaphones rolling, the drums pounding. As the band played a medley of "Coming Round the Mountain," "Shake, Rattle, and Roll," and "Smoke Gets in Your Eyes," she prepared to blow her top. First CO_2 cartridges puffed "smoke" out of her crest; then with a sudden blast of band director Bill Bissell's 12-gauge model shotgun, she exploded, sending band members scattering. So ended the University of Washington's "Salute to Mt. St. Helens," one of the more memorable Bowl halftime shows in recent years.

Whether they honor their school back home or a geological phenomenon, the bands have their own competitions in the Bowl, just as intense as the struggle their teams wage on the gridiron. Joined by their cheerleaders, twirlers, flag bearers, and song girls, they are informally judged and rated. With TV cutting to an overhead blimp shot at any moment, a band's formations need to be absolutely accurate. One player out of step or out of line will stick out. "You're really under the microscope," says one band director. There is no official scoring for the beauty of song leaders, cheerleaders' stunts, or halftime shows, but every squad member knows that his group is being compared to the one from across the field.

Each school will try to do something different to show off. Ohio State spins out its "script Ohio" in duplicate, spelling it out for both sides of the field. USC, which characterizes itself as Hollywood's band, will feature a guest recording artist or the theme from a recent movie. Illinois brings on its mascot Chief Illiniwik to do his traditional war dance. In 1967, Purdue came to the Bowl with the world's biggest drum—unfortunately, it got stuck in one of the Bowl's narrow tunnels, creating a traffic jam for stampeding football players. Stanford has its iconoclastic, brilliant, motley-looking band; USC its classically Californian, blonde tanned song girls; UCLA its card stunts. But which band or which cheerleaders win? From an unbiased viewpoint it's hard to tell. I like the way Arizona State band director Dr. Robert Fleming puts it. "I tell my group," he says, "when you come off the field, if you feel like you did your best, you beat the other band."

STRIKE UP THE BAND

Planning a halftime show for the Bowl presents special challenges. The first thing to take into account is the shape of the Bowl. With its gentle slope and wide lip, it is very dead acoustically. "You feel like you're playing all alone," says one UCLA trombonist. Sound floats right out. Directors tend to choose tunes that stress the brass and dispense with woodwind solos. One director asks his players to aim their horns low, below the level of the tunnels, to contain the sound. The wide shape also makes it difficult to do configurations that will be easily read. Letters work best if they are elongated and pictures if they are stretched out to be seen from an angle. "You don't want people in the stands to wonder what you're making out there," explains one director.

Members of bands marching in the Bowl for the first time cannot rely on familiar landmarks, but have to depend on the grid of the field. Even the location of numbers and hatch marks can vary from the stadium back home. When Michigan comes out to Pasadena, band director Eric Becher recreates the Rose Bowl with chalk, including the figure of the rose in the middle, on their practice field, usually at a local high school.

When it comes to planning shows, the Big Ten bands are at a disadvantage. They have a longer distance to travel, requiring a bigger budget, and because of cold winter weather at home they usually cannot practice outdoors before they come to California. They often bring a show that combines features of their best routines from the fall season, adding a number to herald their presence in sunny California—a Beach Boys song, "California, Here I Come," or maybe a Latin tune. Traditionally, the Big Ten bands are known for marching with high knee lifts, very fast tempos, and almost militaristic precision. In fact, the modified

Competition rages not just on the football field. Below: Ohio State spins out its trademark script "Ohio" in duplicate for both sides of the stadium. An obscure French military march was chosen because the music lasted as long as the routine.

military uniform of the Ohio State band, with the players' white cross belts and spiffy white spats, owes its origins to a time when the band was part of ROTC. The Pac-10 bands have a more eclectic tradition, encompassing everything from the polished mayhem of Stanford to the show biz glitz of USC. Recently, though, the Big Ten has proved just as eclectic, doing a traditional fast tempo pre-game show and then branching out to rock 'n' roll at the half.

At the Rose Bowl each band is allotted seven and a half minutes for its show. The band director chooses formations that enhance the music. Although Dr. Fleming concedes that his ASU fans like to see figures they can recognize, he often favors abstract shapes, like diamonds, circles, squares. When his band played "Jesus Christ Superstar" in the '87 Bowl, he devised a circle that grew, because, as he says, the music said "expand' to him. Some numbers require dance routines. Dr. Arthur Bartner at USC lets his students invent the steps. "They know them. If you went out discoing you'd see them doing them. If I did it, they'd be doing the jitterbug."

Because the USC and UCLA bands do not have to travel very far, they often have the time and the extra funds to perform some of the Bowl's more adventurous shows. In 1983, Jan and Dean were guest stars of the UCLA band, singing, appropriately enough, "Little Old Lady from Pasadena." In 1974, Diana Ross was USC's guest star, performing "Our Love Is Here To Stay" from her film that year "Lady Sings the Blues." In 1985, when Lee Iacocca was the parade's grand marshal, USC brought on a huge inflatable Statue of Liberty that inspired commentary even from the unflappable NBC sports announcers.

In the early 70s, many university bands were doing shows with controversial, politically relevant themes. There was a brouhaha in Ann Arbor when Michigan's student body voted that their band restage their 1971 anti-war homecoming show in the '72 Bowl. In it, the musicians would play Taps as a group of Vietnam veterans released black balloons. The Michigan band and school officials vetoed the idea, but not without the decision being taken to court by the ACLU, where the judge ruled in favor of the school officials. That same year Stanford's band, or "SMUT— Stanford's Marching Unit Thinkers," as they called themselves, made Tournament and TV officials nervous with their penchant for controversy and double entendre. But in the Bowl, the only peace symbols were on the Sousaphones during the parade—not on the field at halftime.

209

Cheerleaders often do stunts that are as physically demanding as the game itself. All the stunts are designed to keep the crowd enthusiastic, to "maintain the momentum."

Below: Fans, especially those who don't get to the Bowl often, are as enthusiastic about the halftime show as they are about the game.
Opposite: Bands of local schools have the time and the funds to perform some of the more adventurous shows.

Bands make special songs their own. Of course, there are the classic fight songs, like "Oskee Wow Wow" or "Buckeye Battle-cry," but sometimes a song written for another purpose becomes associated with a school band. Washington fans expect "Tequila" whenever a touchdown is made. UCLA loves "Twist and Shout." The Ohio State band has been playing "Hang On Sloopy" so long that few remember it was originally a hit with the McCoys. Similarly, they do their trademark "script" Ohio to an obscure French military march, chosen over 50 years ago because its length happened to coincide with the length of the routine. Now, for most fans, "Le Regiment de Sambre et Muse" says OSU—"Like the overture from 'William Tell' has come to be known as the theme from 'The Lone Ranger,'" says past band director Dr. Paul Droste.

In the parade, too, bands choose appropriate songs: "Everything's Coming Up Roses," naturally; "Zippity Doo Dah" to salute the land of Disneyland; or in years gone by, when the bands traveled to California by train, "The Atchinson, Topeka and the Santa Fe," to salute their transportation hosts. As the bands

march down Colorado Boulevard, fans of the Big Ten or Pac-10 cheer their schools and show their respective colors. In 1987, during a lull in the parade, director Dr. Fleming gave the signal for his ASU band members to break formation and greet the enthusiastic crowd. The fans went wild, grabbing them, shaking their hands, giving them cool drinks. When Fleming blew the whistle to call them back, some fans would not let the kids go. "I hate parades," he admits, "but with a crowd like that, I'd do the Rose Parade again in a minute."

THE SPIRIT

Of course, the bands are not the only ones drumming up enthusiasm for their schools. The cheerleaders are part of the parade too, jumping off their float to lead the grandstands in an organized cheer, doing flips and handsprings on the asphalt, following their mascots—the duck, the bear, the buckeye—down the rose-colored line. Jo and Josephine Bruin distinguish UCLA from its erstwhile parent school, Cal Berkeley, and Cal's ferocious golden bears. Illinois's Chief Illiniwek marches in his authentic

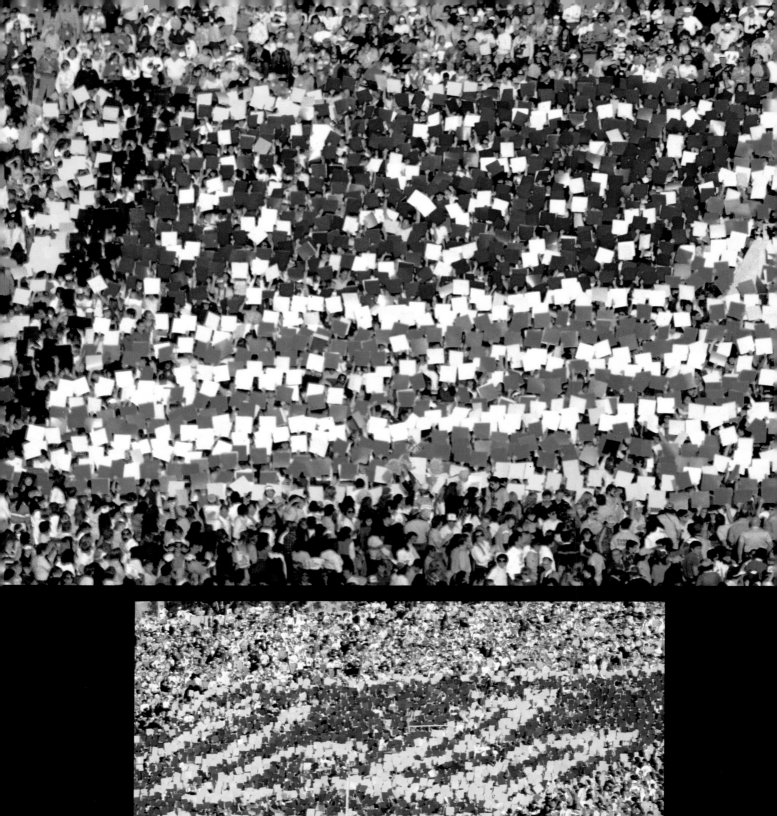

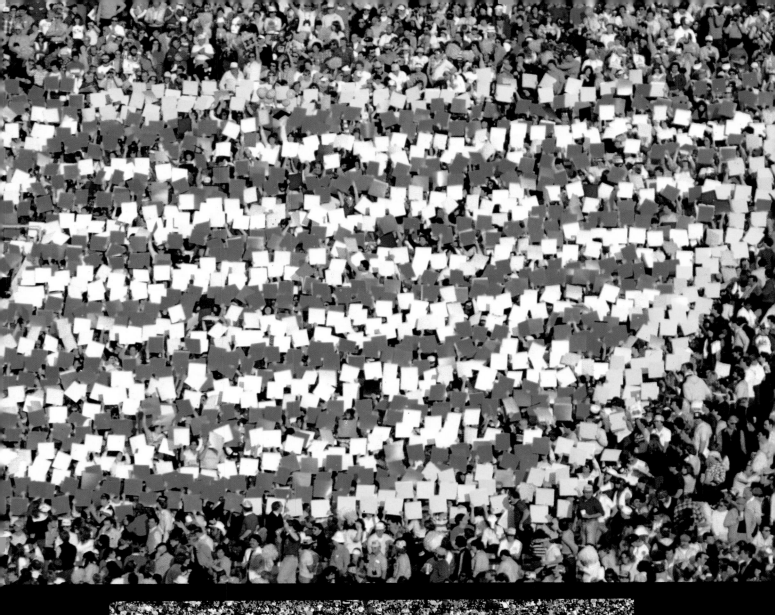

Indian attire—although there has never been an Illini tribe besides the one on the gridiron.

At the Bowl, the cheerleaders do stunts that are as physically demanding as the game itself: partner stunts with girls flipping off of the guys' shoulders, running broad jumps over rows of kneeling cheerleaders, somersaults, handsprings, back handsprings, and double flips. Of course, keeping up the crowd's enthusiasm is key. "You've got to keep the momentum on your side," says one cheerleader. Sometimes that means organized yells, like "Let's Go, Blue," or a spell-out such as "S-O-U-T-H-E-R-N-C-A-L-I-F-O-R-N-I-A." At other times, cheerleaders just want the crowd to keep up the noise, urging them, "Okay, this is their fourth down with only a yard to go, let's get rolling." Or they take out their car keys and shake them, inspiring the fans to the same.

One recent phenomenon has been "the wave," in which Bowl fans stand up and raise their hands in a wave that moves around the stadium, like the Rockettes kicking in an undulating row. No one can say for sure who introduced it to the Bowl, but there is evidence that it originated at the University of Washington, where it was introduced at the 1982 homecoming by former cheerleader Rob Weller, currently a host on TV's "Entertainment Tonight."

The cheerleaders also get support from organized card sections, most notably UCLA's. Situated on the sunny side of the Bowl, between tunnels five, six, and seven, the UCLA card section comprises 3,176 seats rising from row 13 to row 52. Each student is given five cards, with a different color on each side, and at their seat they discover their directions—placed there earlier and carefully guarded against sabotage. During halftime the stunts are called by numbers, sometimes by rank or row to give special moving effects, like champagne pouring out of a bottle or the American flag unfurling. UCLA is wont to salute anything from Hollywood movies, the Pac-10, NBC (to be sure they are on camera) to moms, spelling out "Hi Mom!" But they always end with their signature, UCLA.

A TRIP TO FILMVILLE

For the bands and cheerleaders travelling long distances to Pasadena, the trip is undeniably glamorous. "When we were out there," says '82 Iowa cheerleader Rick Justis, "we practiced on the UCLA track, right across the street from the entrance to Bel Air. We'd always keep one eye on the gate. If somebody said, 'There goes Johnny Carson,' we would have believed him. Most of us were from the Midwest, and that was our first time out to California . . . We called it 'Filmville.' " The Iowa squad, like most bands and cheerleaders, went to Disneyland, Universal Studios, Farmer's Market, Knotts Berry Farm. They held a pep rally for the thousands of fans who had come out from Iowa with them. They went to the beach at Venice and watched the muscular, tanned roller-skating queens. They tried to pick up a few girls at a Westwood club. They toured several TV studios and met producers. "The whole thing was like Disneyland," Justis remembers. "It was cold that year, maybe in the 50s, and everybody said, Sorry about the weather.' We said, 'You should be in Iowa.' I mean, we practiced out there in shorts and T-shirts!"

There is a headiness about the whole experience. "Some of our kids had never even been to a big city," James Hile, assistant director of the Illinois band, says of their '84 trip. Dr. Paul Droste, who took his Ohio State band out to six Rose Bowls, says, "After you've been to Pasadena a number of times, you remember how nice all the people are." Probably the most eventful visit for him was when the truck to haul the band's Sousaphones never showed up on the morning of the parade. "We were staying on the UCLA campus at the time . . . We waited 45 minutes. Finally, a guy drove by in a U-Haul truck and we told him, 'We need your truck.' 'Oh, fine,' he said. Then in Pasadena, we drove the wrong way down a one-way street. The police stopped us until we explained, 'We're the Ohio State band!' We got to the parade with only minutes to spare."

"It's a helluvalong day," says Justis. "We had to be ready to go at five or six in the morning. It was too exciting to sleep anyway. At the Bowl, we couldn't wait to do pushups in the end zone—we do them whenever Iowa scores. One for each point. As it turned out, we never got to do them in the Rose Bowl.

"At the end of the game, the crowd was yelling and screaming and on their feet. We all looked pretty bad. The girls' hair was shot, our sweaters were trashed. We had paint stains, from what they paint the field with, all over. I remember we had purple footprints, from Washington's colors, on our shoulders. We lost, but everybody was still excited. 'We're in the Rose Bowl,' we kept saying. We went out to the center of the field, standing on top of the rose, taking pictures. We didn't leave the stadium for an hour and a half. The lights went out. 'We may get locked in here,' we said. We didn't care. We were still so excited. We were in the Rose Bowl."

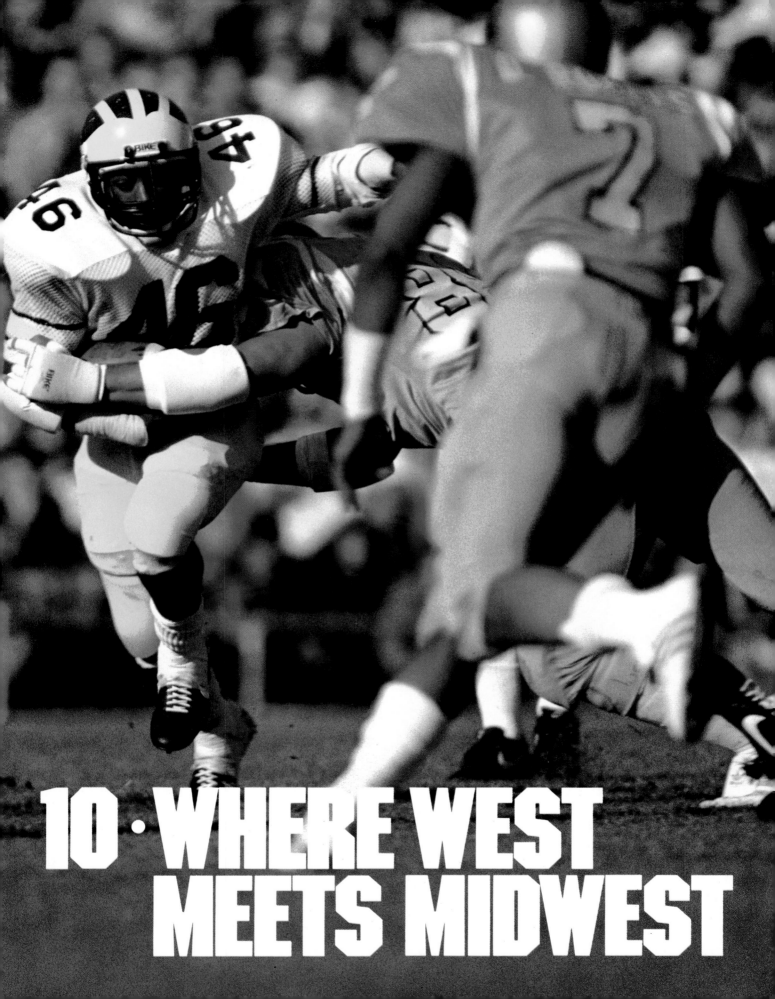

10 · WHERE WEST MEETS MIDWEST

In 1984 when the University of Illinois came out to the Rose Bowl for the first time in 20 years, 25,000 fans followed them. Tribes of Illini took over the Bonaventure in downtown L.A., the Century Plaza in Century City, the Beverly Wilshire in Beverly Hills, the Airport Hyatt, the Huntington Sheraton in Pasadena, and thousands of convertible sofas in between. Wherever they camped, halls that had recently seen boughs of holly were hung with orange and blue—banners, crepe paper, balloons—and images of Santa replaced by Chief Illiniwek. Back in Champaign Urbana, retailers were selling out of anything bearing a rose: shirts, hats, ties, mufflers (for the cold of the Midwest only), special Coca Cola bottles with Chief Illiniwek on one side and the Tournament logo on the other. People bought red roses as though it were Valentine's Day.

In Hollywood, the Big Ten Dinner of Champions at the Palladium had an unprecedented 2,500 guests (after turning away another 1,000), and broadcast the festivities live for the less fortunate in Chicago. No matter that this was the team some Illinois journalists were dubbing "the University of California at Champaign Urbana" because so many of its players came from the Golden State—the fans could not be fooled. In one vast migration, the Corn Belt moved to the Sun Belt, Illinois took over California.

The Rose Bowl does not belong to any one team. Of course, it has hosted Super Bowls, Olympic soccer matches, junior college games, and UCLA for home games (Walter O'Malley even briefly considered it for the Dodgers). But it's the game played on January 1 that gives the Bowl its name and mystique. It's a perpetual trophy, as grand a tradition as the America's Cup, waiting to be etched with a new victor's name. Each year when the top Big Ten team and top Pac-10 team come to town they woo it with pompoms, warpaint, pennants, pep rallies, and ceremonial dinners that make Homecoming in Madison, or Pullman, look like a church picnic.

"Lemmings do not race any more blindly for the sea than Buckeye fans toward Pasadena," said Jerry Brondfield, the Ohio State University football historian about the Columbus migration that accompanies any OSU Rose Bowl bid, even when it looks like an annual event, as it did in the '70s. The migration mushrooms in size when the bid goes to a school, like Illinois, that has not smelled the roses for decades. In 1982, when Iowa played in Pasadena for the first time since 1959, 40,000 Hawkeye fans made the trek to Southern California, so many that the governor suggested, "Last one out turn off the lights." Iowa alums who had settled in L.A. suddenly heard from long-lost pals they barely remembered. Again and again they had to answer the question, "Do you have any extra tickets?" When Arizona State made its first Bowl appearance in 1987, one often-quoted fan was asked if he would drive to Pasadena. "No," he remarked, "I'll save on gas. There will be so many motorhomes lined up between here and there, I'll just walk across the tops of them."

In 1978, Washington Governor Dixy Lee Ray came down with an entourage of RVs and motorhomes, parking her own near the Rose Bowl where she could walk her pet poodle Jacques, an unlikely Husky fan. In 1961, there was a near-riot in Columbus when Ohio State's faculty council voted against sending the Buckeyes to Pasadena. They had won the Big Ten that year and had been invited to the Bowl, but the faculty felt that athletics were being overemphasized, to the detriment of academics, and the Buckeyes had to wait for another chance. It took a stirring speech by the team's co-captain that year, Mike Ingram, to quell the angry campus crowds.

Even for schools that have not played in Pasadena in years, the Bowl retains its allure. From Berkeley to Bloomington, wherever a Big Ten or Pac-10 team has a promising game, the fans start chanting, "Rose Bowl, Rose Bowl!" I recently watched Northwestern, the perpetual Big Ten underdogs, obliterate a much worse (and non-conference) Princeton team. By the third quarter, when the Princeton Tigers had failed to score a point against the Wildcats, Northwestern was taking up the unlikely cheer, "Rose Bowl, Rose Bowl!" Representing the Tournament at an Ohio State pep rally before their season-deciding game against Michigan, Fred Soldwedel said the 20,000 Buckeye fans gave the Cotton Bowl representative a modest reception. "But when I was introduced they couldn't stop clapping and cheering and yelling, 'Rose Bowl, Rose Bowl!'" After all, the former Bowl would be a consolation prize, but the latter would be the spoils of victory.

A MATCH IS MADE

And yet, it was not always so for the Big Ten. Michigan played in the first Bowl game in 1902 and Ohio State came out in 1921, but after they were beaten by one of Cal's so-called "wonder teams" (28-0), the Big Ten made a rule against *any* post-season Bowl games. The conference said it was because they did not want college football to be overemphasized, but many in the West suspected they feared another defeat. For the next few decades,

selection of the teams to play in the Bowl remained remarkably casual.

In those days, the Tournament chose a representative from the West and one from the East; the two teams met in Pasadena and then went home. Then in the mid-30s, the Tournament happily handed the selection process over to the Pacific Coast Conference (as the Pac-10 was known then). They sent their champion team and selected an Eastern or Southern or Midwestern team to compete against it in the Bowl. This worked relatively well until the mid-40s when competition from other Bowl games had increased. With the Cotton, Sugar, and Orange Bowls each looking for the champions from their own regions (and often under political pressures making it difficult for the schools to say no), it was harder to get the top Southern team or one from Texas in the Rose Bowl. But by then, the Big Ten was softening its ban on post-season games and the Tournament was ready to reconsider the Midwest.

The two conferences looked like a good match. The schools had similarly high academic standards, equally strong athletic programs and thousands of loyal alumni. In fact, after the

Substitute halfback for UCLA, Al Hoisch races for the end zone to become the first player in Rose Bowl history to return a kickoff for a touchdown. The play covered 103 yards.

Pac-10, the Big Ten has more graduates living in Southern California than any other conference. Moreover, the Big Ten schools were in the population center of the United States and the Tournament already had its eye on the potential of a large cross-country television audience.

In 1946 the Tournament issued its invitation. The Big Ten (or as it was known then, the Big Nine) hesitated. It wanted some conditions, such as a no-repeat rule that no Big Ten team could play in the Bowl two years in a row (a ruling abandoned only in the 70s) and still it could not make up its mind. What finally decided the conference was the public clamoring to see a very strong Army team—*not* a Big Ten team—play in the 1947 Rose Bowl. *Now*, there was some competition. The Big Ten accepted the bid and the best teams from the two conferences have played every year in the Bowl since.

It has not always been a popular decision. Initially, the Tournament was criticized for turning the Bowl into "a closed shop." Former Rose Bowl players, such as the star of the '26 game, Alabaman Johnny Mack Brown, objected to limiting the honor. "It should be spread around," he said. By 1951, a group of college

223

presidents brought up a motion at the NCAA convention to cancel *all* post-season Bowl games. They felt college athletics were being overemphasized (clearly, a recurring complaint). The motion was tabled only after much pleading from Tournament representatives Lay Leishman, William Nicholas, and John Biggar, Sr. In the early years of the pact, when for 13 years the West Coast representatives won only once, people claimed it was an unbalanced match. Now after a long period of dominance by the Pac-10, people make the same criticism.

There have been complaints that the balmy weather saps the strength of the teams coming from colder climes (one losing coach wryly complained that his team ate too many oranges) and protests that the natural grass in the Bowl presents an unfair advantage to the Pac-10 teams (all but one Big Ten stadiums are carpeted in artificial turf) and grumblings that the Midwesterners are too easily distracted by the sights and sun of Southern California (although that could also be said of some faraway Pac-10 schools like Washington and Oregon State). Still, over 40 years after the pact's inauguration, no one can argue with its success.

Before the pact went into effect, there were only five sold-out games. Since 1947, every game has been a sellout. About 50,000 tickets go to the Pac-10, 26,000 to the Big Ten, and the remainder to the Tournament. The Rose Bowl has continually attracted huge crowds from the Midwest to Southern California. And the income from a combination of gate receipts, program sales, concession sales, and media rights, has helped *all* the athletic programs of the Pac-10 and Big Ten schools.

In an arrangement that does more than just reward the Bowl invitees, the revenues are split three ways. After the expenses of putting on the game are covered, the Tournament takes 15% (a large portion of which goes to the City of Pasadena). The remaining 85% is divided in half between the Pac-10 and Big Ten. First, each conference covers the costs of sending the teams out to California—footing hotel bills, food bills, the cost of new equipment, and transportation. Then the pie is divided again, 10 ways in the Pac-10 and 11 ways in the Big Ten (the extra slice goes to the Big Ten office). In effect each school gets a no-strings-attached grant to its athletic department.

"It's income we can count on," says Chris Voelz, associate athletic director from the University of Oregon. "That's very helpful when we're drawing up our budget." Other sources of funds are less predictable. Local gate receipts and concessions can change with a winning or losing season, but every year the

Opposite: Coach Lynn "Pappy" Waldorf brought his California Bears to the Rose Bowl three consecutive years starting in 1949.

Above: The 1956 game pitted a UCLA powerhouse against an equally formidable Michigan squad. The game, tied 14-14 in the fourth quarter, was decided in favor of Michigan on a field goal.

Left: Duffy Daugherty, Michigan's coach. It was Daugherty's decision to let Dave Kaiser kick the winning field goal against UCLA despite the fact Kaiser hadn't kicked in two months.

225

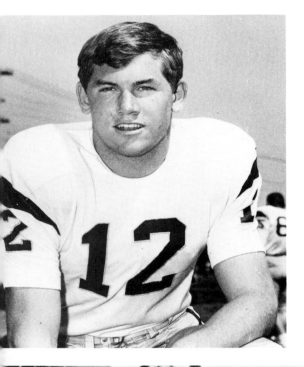

schools in the Pac-10 and Big Ten can expect several hundred thousand dollars from the Rose Bowl. Those funds do not just go to underwrite football either. They support track and swimming and women's basketball and volleyball. "We've got 18 sports and 16 of them lose money," says Harold Mauro, assistant athletic director at the University of Indiana. The benefits are spread around.

Ever since the Big Ten and Pac-10 have been meeting annually on the first of January, the Bowl has hosted triumphant national champs, underrated underdogs, top-ranked teams who prove they deserve even better rankings, and disappointed squads with little to say in postgame press conferences. The best of the West faces the best of the Midwest on the gridiron, with resultant draws, shutouts, and close calls. Here are the highlights of some of those games.

1947: THE START OF SOMETHING BIG

UCLA was favored to beat Illinois in the 1947 Bowl. They were undefeated that year, outscoring their opponents 216 to 45, while the Illini had lost two games. UCLA had hoped to play the highly rated Army team in the Bowl and they assumed that meeting any other team would be a romp. But they had not taken the talents of Buddy Young into account.

As unlikely a football player as you can imagine, Claude "Buddy" Young stood only 5'4" and weighed a mere 155 pounds. When he went professional, he was the smallest man ever to play pro football. Although he was not the first black to star in the Bowl (that honor goes to Fritz Pollard of Brown University who played in Pasadena back in 1916), he was one of the first blacks to break the color barrier in pro football. He grew up in Chicago in a large family presided over by a mother who had played basketball and volleyball in her youth. She encouraged her son and recognized his talent as a runner. At a time when the world record for the 100-yard dash was 9.4, Buddy Young could do it in 9.5 seconds. In football he ran so fast his opponents hardly had time to see him, let alone tackle him. As Frankie Albert told sportswriters Herb Michelson and Dave Newhouse, "Defensive linemen lived in fear of making an error, because once he got behind you he was a blur."

In the Rose Bowl that year, Illinois scored early, after only seven plays. UCLA, gingerly avoiding Buddy Young, came back with a touchdown later in the first quarter. But then Illinois

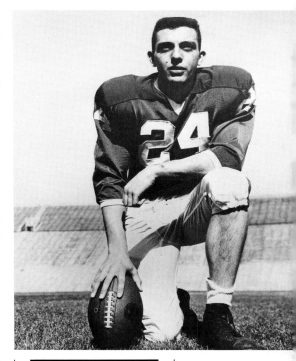

The 1963 Rose Bowl game between Wisconsin and USC was perhaps the greatest offensive display in Tournament history. It featured the quarterbacking of Pete Beathard (opposite top left) and Ron VanderKelen (above). Although USC won, the game was in doubt as VanderKelen brought Wisconsin back in the fourth quarter. The game lasted long enough to induce the Rose Bowl to improve the stadium lighting.

227

unleashed Young. On a spread formation, the Illini quarterback flipped the ball to halfback Young deep in the backfield where he could build up the momentum to cross the line at top speed. He made 16 yards on the play and scored a touchdown several plays later, leaving UCLA out of breath and finally so demoralized that they would never catch up. Ironically, though, the game's most exciting play belonged to UCLA.

In the second quarter, Bruin halfback Al Hoish caught an Illinois kickoff three yards into his own end zone. Weighing just 139 pounds, Hoish was a substitute halfback, but when he caught the ball, instead of prudently downing it, he ran. He skirted a few tacklers, picked up blocking from his teammates, dodged an Illini defender in midfield, and streaked straight into the end zone on an amazing 103-yard touchdown run.

Several years later, the UCLA coach Bert LaBrucherie had a few disclaimers to make about the game. "Had we been duly forewarned as to the strength of Big Ten teams, and with a favorable psychological situation, we still believe this would have been a whale of a game. The bad psychological situation arose when Army . . . was shunted aside with inauguration of the pact with the Big Ten. The team, after reading the Los Angeles papers, evidently considered Illinois a pushover. May I say that this feeling was not shared by the coaching staff, as we feared and respected our Midwest opponent." After they lost, 45-14 perhaps that respect increased.

For the next dozen years, the Pac-10 teams could rarely give the excuse that they were overconfident in the Bowl. Routings by the Big Ten came to be expected. In 1948, a respectable team from USC was destroyed by the University of Michigan, 49-0, a score that recalled the U of M's first and only previous visit to Pasadena in 1902. In 1949, Coach Lynn "Pappy" Waldorf brought his California Bears to the Bowl for the first of three consecutive visits. Each time the Bears lost, and in each case only in the fourth quarter after gaining hopeful leads. USC finally won one for the Pac-10 when they beat Wisconsin, 7-0, in 1953 (a game then vice-president-elect Richard Nixon reviewed as the Tournament's grand marshal). But after that, the Pac-10 went back to losing. The turnaround didn't really come until the next decade, although there were moments when the West Coast conference put up a good fight.

The 1966 game was coach Tommy Prothro's (opposite left) first as Bruin coach, and Gary Beban's sophomore year at quarterback. The highlight of the game came when Bob Stiles (opposite right) knocked himself out stopping fullback Bob Apisa from scoring a two-point conversion.

1956: DOWN TO THE WIRE

The 1954 UCLA Bruins should have played in the 1955 Bowl. They were voted national champions in the UPI polls that year and their coach, Red Sanders, coach of the year. But because they had been to the Bowl the previous year, falling to Michigan State, 28-20, they were out of the running. (In those days, the Pacific Coast Conference, like the Big Ten, had a no-repeat clause in their Rose Bowl agreement.) Southern California, which had lost 34-0 to UCLA, went to the Bowl instead, and were soundly defeated by Woody Hayes's Ohio State team, 20-7.

UCLA had to wait until 1956 to return to the Bowl, and that year they were rated fourth in the polls. They faced a bigger, tougher-looking Michigan State team, with, as one Bruin put it later, "lots of boom up there in the line." The Spartans were number two in the nation and featured All-American quarterback and future professional star Earl Morrall. Still, the mighty Bruins gave Michigan a scare right on the first play. As Michigan State coach Duffy Daugherty later described it, "In setting up our opening sequence, I decided on a first down pass because I figured the Bruins would be charged up and give with a big rush. So we passed, they intercepted and then they scored." It was not going to be an easily settled contest.

For the rest of the game the two teams seemed to growl at each other as they inched towards one goal line or the other. Michigan State tied the score in the second quarter. Then in the fourth, the Spartans scored again when end John Lewis caught a pass from halfback Clarence Peaks and ran it into the end zone. UCLA came back, pushing down the field, with substitute fullback Doug Peters taking the ball over the goal line. The score was tied again, 14-14, and the ball back in the Spartans' hands.

They moved down the field, and with over a minute and a half left, tried to break the tie with a field goal. Their placekicker Gerry Plautis booted one from the UCLA 22-yard line. But he missed and the ball went back to the Bruins.

On their first play, the Bruins were penalized for coaching from the sidelines when an assistant coach made a passing motion to the quarterback Ronnie Knox. On second down, they were penalized again for having an ineligible receiver downfield (and the fans started wondering if anybody could break the tie). On third down, from the 1-yard line, Knox tried to quick-kick, but the ball hardly traveled, ending up in Michigan State's possession on the Bruin 19-yard line.

The 1971 Bowl game appeared to be a mismatch —Ohio State, loser of one game in three years vs. Stanford, loser of three in one year. But Jim Plunkett (opposite), no stranger to adversity, led the Indians, coached by John Ralston (above), to a surprising 27-17 victory.

231

Opposite and below: The 1975 game boasted a USC defense that limited Heisman great Archie Griffin (45) to 76 yards, the first time in 23 games that he had failed to gain over 100.
Right: Pad Haden directed the offense, which included a last-minute conversion pass which won the game.

The Spartans had as much trouble scoring as the Bruins. They fumbled twice, recovered twice, received a penalty for illegal use of hands,and with only seconds left, kicked from the 24-yard line. This time sophomore end Dave Kaiser went in for the honors (after Plautis had failed in two previous efforts). Apparently he had never successfully kicked a field goal in either a college or high school game, but the Spartans were willing to try *anything*. Kaiser was the right choice. He booted the ball 41 yards, splitting the uprights, and the Spartans scored another victory (albeit a close one) for the Big Ten, 17-14.

1963: A FOOTBALL SPECTACULAR

The University of Southern California came to the Bowl in 1963 with their first perfect season since the 1930s—no defeats, no ties, and a number-one ranking in the AP and UPI polls. In ten games that season Southern Cal had only given up 55 points. Meeting them that year was the University of Wisconsin, like the Trojans the unexpected victors in their conference. Wisconsin had won all but one of its regular season games, finishing the year ranked number two in the nation. Perhaps the biggest surprise that year had been the performance of the Wisconsin quarterback, Ron VanderKelen. A third-string quarterback the previous year, VanderKelen was given the top position by virtue of experience. He ended up leading the league in total offense with 1,237 yards. Although Wisconsin was rated number two behind USC, most experts expected they would win by a few points; the Big Ten was considered a tougher conference. But for three quarters the experts were proved wrong.

It was a long game. It started fifteen minutes late; halftime went on an extra ten because of the bands' elaborate shows. One referee also seemed to be putting on a show of his own, signaling extravagantly for the TV cameras (it was the second time the game had been televised in color nationwide). And USC was very methodical about scoring touchdowns. At the end of the first half they led, 21-7.

There was a brief altercation when VanderKelen, carrying the ball, was pushed over the bench out of bounds on the Wisconsin side by USC defensive end Hal Bedsole. Bedsole barely made it back to his own side alive. In the second half, Bedsole retaliated by running down the sidelines (making sure he was in front of the USC benches) for a 57-yard scoring play. At the top of the fourth quarter USC scored its sixth touchdown, a pass from quarterback

Pete Beathard, *his* fourth touchdown toss of the day (a Rose Bowl record). With only 14 minutes left in the game, USC was ahead, 42-14. The crowds headed for the exits, darkness was descending. But the game was not over . . . yet.

VanderKelen came alive. In that one quarter he threw 21 passes (he completed 33 out of 48 attempts in the game, both Rose Bowl records). He could do no wrong. He passed in the air, from the ground—once even after colliding with an official. Almost every time a teammate caught the ball. With the minutes running out, Wisconsin kept scoring. Finally, between USC and Wisconsin, so many balls were kicked into the stands on field goals and conversions the Tournament ran out of footballs. Someone had to retrieve a practice ball out of the USC locker room. With more than a minute left to go, Wisconsin had scored 23 points. They were seemingly within inches of USC, 42-37. They got the ball, time for one more play, one more touchdown . . . and then the gun went off.

Who knows what might have happened? USC trudged off the field feeling more relieved than elated. And Wisconsin, with every reason to feel disappointed, could only echo their coach, Milt Bruhn, "What I wouldn't give for one minute more!"

1966: DAVID TAKES GOLIATH

The 1966 Rose Bowl was not the first time UCLA had met Michigan State. They had played each other that September in the season opener in East Lansing, and the strapping Spartans defeated the Bruins, 13-3. Michigan State continued to win every game they played, gaining a reputation for an impenetrable defensive line, dubbed "The Great Wall of Sparta." In their regular season games they held their opponents to a stingy average of 45.6 rushing yards per game. The team boasted seven All-Americans, including six-foot eight-inch, 287-pound defensive end Bubba Smith, whose sheer size was enough to strike fear in the heart of any opponent.

Michigan State was ranked number one in the UPI poll and tied for number one in the AP poll. Still, their coach, Duffy Daugherty, was not taking chances when he brought his team out to Pasadena. Perhaps he recalled Michigan State's narrow victory over UCLA in the Rose Bowl ten years earlier, when the Spartans won by a 41-yard field goal in the final seconds of the game. For several nights before the '66 game Daugherty kept his Spartans hidden from the press in a monastery in the foothills

Above: 102,594 fans watched USC outduel Ohio State, 20-17, in 1985. Co-players of the game were Jack Del Rio and Tim Green.
Opposite: The running of tailback Alan Dial couldn't dampen the spirits of 25,000 Illinois fans who trekked westward to see their team in the Rose Bowl for the first time in twenty years.

above town. Security at practices was so tight that on one occasion even Daugherty could not get in.

UCLA that year was young, inexperienced, and willing to take any risk to win. It was Tommy Prothro's first year coaching the Bruins. Previously he had been with Oregon State (whom he had brought to the Bowl in '65) and not too many years before that he had played in the Rose Bowl himself. UCLA starting quarterback Gary Beban was only a sophomore. Playing left defensive tackle was a young man who would eventually see some good years in the Rose Bowl, future UCLA coach Terry Donahue.

L.A. sportswriter Jim Murray compared the imminent spectacle to "feeding Christians to lions." UCLA was expected to lose by two or three touchdowns—and suffer a lot of crushed bones. In a recent *L.A. Times* article, Prothro recalled giving a pep talk saying, "Relax, there are 300 million Chinese who wouldn't give a damn if we won or lost." His players, on the other hand, were ready to spit nails, especially when they heard the Spartans shouting as they warmed up, "We'll show those surfer boys."

On the game's first offensive play UCLA quarterback Gary Beban ran for 27 yards, just so the Spartans would know UCLA meant business. Early in the second quarter, the "surfer boys" scored, after recovering a fumble on the Michigan State 6. Beban scored again, this time after the Bruins recovered their own onside kick. Both of the points after touchdown were good, and amazingly, the Bruins were leading at the half, 14-0.

It was not until the middle of the third quarter that Michigan State made a comeback. Three times UCLA was able to stop them on fourth down with a yard to go. Finally, though, the Spartans scored—although the point after touchdown was not good. Then in the fourth quarter they scored again, making it 14-12, with only 31 seconds left in the game. Michigan State had only one choice; they had to go for a two-point run in hopes of tying the game. 212-pound fullback Bob Apisa, the "Bull," would take the ball across the goal line. When he got there, though, he was greeted by five-foot, nine-inch, 175-pound UCLA defensive back Bob Stiles, who threw himself at Apisa so hard that he knocked himself out. But he stopped Apisa from scoring, and in one of the biggest upsets in Rose Bowl history, UCLA beat Michigan State, 14-12.

It was the first time that UCLA won in the Bowl. Since then, they have not lost.

1971-1972: CALIFORNIA CASUAL

The irreverent Stanford band seemed to symbolize what was wrong with Stanford. They did not march in militaristic formation time; rather they scurried like fieldmice from location to location, their long hair trailing behind them like the long hair that peeked out from under Stanford's football helmets. In the parade they wore dozens of different hats, beanies, boaters, fishing hats, seemingly unaware that Ohio's Marine-style marching band, where everyone looked the same, was usually the standard. Even their drum-major did things differently, pedalling a tricycle on the field and conducting wearing an oversized diaper. But when they played brassy pop tunes from bands like Chicago and Blood, Sweat and Tears, suddenly all the mastery behind Ohio State's precision drilling was momentarily eclipsed.

When Stanford came to the Bowl in '71 and '72, they were a little hard to take seriously. Their amiable coach John Ralston with his open, slap-you-on-the-back manner was such a nice guy that even curmudgeon Woody Hayes liked him. His players did not look like Ohio and Michigan's beefy, corn-fed, steel-mill kids. They were philosophy and psychology majors, pre-med students and pre-law scholars. They did not even have very impressive records. In 1971 Ohio had lost only one game in three years; Stanford had lost three in one year. In 1972, Michigan had scored 421 points, almost a point a minute, in a perfect season; Stanford's record that year was a flawed 8-3.

But Stanford was always doing the unexpected—like their band. In the Bowl they capitalized on the psychological advantage of being underdogs and their own exaggerated reputation for nonchalance. Then they surprised their opponents with a well-executed aerial game. With pro prospect Jim Plunkett quarterbacking in 1971, Stanford beat Ohio State, 27-17, their first Rose Bowl win in 30 years. When Michigan came out the following year, fans from Ann Arbor were hoping for a replay of their 1902 game, when Michigan destroyed an ill-prepared Stanford team. But this time they were destined to be disappointed.

In the first three quarters, both teams scored only one field goal each. Then early in the fourth quarter, Michigan made a touchdown that put them in the lead, 10-3. Stanford responded by taking a big risk: at fourth and ten on their own 33-yard-line, they faked a punt. The play worked and started Stanford on a drive that culminated in a touchdown, tying the score at 10-10. Then Michigan pushed downfield where they attempted a field

238

goal. The 46-yard kick was short and caught by Stanford sophomore Jim Ferguson, who tried to run it out, but was tackled
behind the goal line, giving Michigan a safety and the lead, 12-10.

Stanford had the ball on their own 22-yard line, with only
1:48 left. Quarterback Don Bunce completed five consecutive
passes, advancing the ball to the Michigan 14. The clock was
stopped, and in stepped the Stanford kicker Rod Garcias. Coach
Jim Ralston had given him an encouraging word before each of
five failed field goal kicks in a game that season against San Jose.
"Coach, don't say anything to Rod this time," one of the players
wisely said. He did not.

With 12 seconds left in the game, Garcias kicked a 31-yard
field goal. And Stanford did it again, beating Michigan, 13-12.

1975: A FAMILY AFFAIR

Even as far back as 1970, Coach Bo Schembechler objected,
"McKay has the Rose Bowl on USC's schedule every year." For his
part, McKay, when asked if he saw anything wrong with the
same teams appearing in the Rose Bowl year after year, quickly
responded, "Yes, I do. I don't think Ohio State should come every
year." In 1975, USC was making its seventh Bowl appearance in
ten years and Ohio State its fifth in ten. For the third consecutive
time one end zone would be painted the Buckeyes' red and grey
and the other the Trojans' cardinal and gold. For the fourth year it
would be the wry, even-tempered McKay vs. the fiery, unpredictable Woody Hayes. One year it had been a victory for USC when
fullback Sam "Bam" Cunningham ran for four touchdowns, a
Rose Bowl record; the next year Ohio State enjoyed sweet revenge
when they trounced the Trojans, 42-21. So far it was two for
Woody and one for McKay.

During the game the two teams were at their defensive
best. USC held Heisman Trophy winner Archie Griffin to only 76
yards, the first time in 23 games that he had failed to gain over 100
yards rushing. In the first quarter, USC kicked a field goal and in
the second Ohio State garnered a touchdown, but there was no
more scoring until the final quarter.

There were some odd moments, though, including an
oddball punt from USC's Jim Lucas. Evidently his foot only
grazed the ball, which hit the ground and bounced in front of
him. Bemused, Lucas picked the ball up and ran 16 yards for an
important first down. While the officials were arguing over
whether it was a punt or a fumble or a straight running play, USC

Opposite: UCLA's Doug West,
Craig Rutledge, and Tommy
Taylor celebrate fumble
recovery against Illinois.
Above: ASU quarterback Jeff
Van Raaphorst, Player of the
Game in 1987, threw for 193
yards and two touchdowns.

241

was counting its good fortune, "I have decided to change our punter into a running back," McKay later said. "The way he moved with the one he missed was our best run of the day."

McKay was exaggerating only slightly. Losing their star running back Anthony Davis to an injury in the second quarter, USC had to depend more on its passing and the teamwork of quarterback Pat Haden and receiver John McKay, the coach's son. The younger McKay had been catching Haden's passes for eight years, going back to high school days, when Haden had boarded with the McKay family. During the game, Haden made some of the best passes of his career. In the fourth quarter he threw to tight end Jim Obravich for USC's first touchdown. This gain was eclipsed when Ohio State came back with a touchdown, and then a field goal, putting the Buckeyes back in the lead, 17-10. Taking control again, Haden systematically moved the ball down the field, the drive culminating with his thrilling 38-yard touchdown pass to his old buddy John McKay.

"Pat and I have fantasized about something like this happening since we were old enough to start watching the Rose Bowl," McKay said. "We always wondered how great it would be to throw and catch a TD pass in the last minutes of the Rose Bowl." Haden, when asked how many times he had thrown the same pass to McKay, replied, "at last count, one million, two-hundred and thirty-seven thousand."

Haden's work was not over yet. The score was 17-16 with less than two minutes left and Haden had to pass again, this time to Shelton Diggs for a two-point conversion (Coach McKay would not be satisfied with a tie). The pass was good and USC won. All a disgruntled Woody could say was, "We got beaten by a better team. One point better."

1983, 1984, 1986: UCLA AT HOME

In the early 80s UCLA seemed to make the Rose Bowl part of their regular season. They might have felt especially at home in Pasadena because the stadium had literally become their home field—since 1982 UCLA home games have been played in the Rose Bowl. If so, on January 1 they never sauntered into the Bowl with the arrogance of sure winners showing off in their living room. They came politely, deferentially, sometimes feigning surprise that they were even asked, acting as if they really believed they were the underdogs everyone said they were. After all, they *were* last-minute invitees in 1983, and in 1984 they *had* started the season with three losses and one tie, and Iowa *did* look awfully strong in 1986. And yet, UCLA won each time.

Nothing seemed to get them down. In 1983 they faced Michigan for the third time in a year. There had been one loss to Michigan, 33-14, in the Bluebonnet Bowl; one close win, 31-27, in Ann Arbor that September; and then there was a solid victory in the Bowl on New Year's Day, 24-14, just to settle the score. Coach Terry Donahue once said that there is "only this much difference" (holding his hands an inch apart) between winning and losing teams. It was as though UCLA took their coach's philosophy to heart.

When UCLA came to Pasadena in 1984, quarterback Rick Neuheisel and seven of his other teammates woke up with food poisoning—not the best condition in which to meet a fourth-ranked Illinois team. "It was really ugly," he later said. Neuheisel and his stricken teammates were driven to the Bowl in private cars so they would not get any sicker. But when Neuheisel started playing, throwing pass after pass, ultimately tying the Rose Bowl record for touchdowns in the air, Illionis was stunned. "I felt fine once I started playing," Neuheisel explained. "The only time I felt sick was when I sat on the bench." Illinois was obliterated, 45-9.

By 1986, Iowa's coach Hayden Fry had wised up to UCLA's "ah shucks, who, us in the Rose Bowl?" tactic. He was not to be fooled. In what he called "Operation No Frills," he flew his team into the less-traveled Ontario airport, installed them in hotel rooms in the distant Industry Hills Sheraton, and kept them away from the sight-seeing distractions of Disneyland, Universal Studios, and the Beef Bowl at Lawry's restaurant, where traditionally the teams have gorged on all the prime rib they can eat. Even when Iowa lost to UCLA, 45-28, Fry said, "Do you realize what the score would have been if we would have let them have fun, if they had been out all night long honky-tonking?" There was no answer to the question.

UCLA made the win look like it was another rabbit they had pulled out of a hat. Their quarterback Matt Stevens was a substitute who had learned only two days before the game that he would be starting. Their tailback Eric Ball was only a second-string freshman, replacing Gaston Green who pulled a leg muscle in the second quarter. That same freshman ended up rushing for four touchdowns, tying Neil Snow's Rose Bowl record set back in 1902. "I didn't know who he was," Hayden Fry said about Ball, "they were all running by me so fast." When it came time to receive accolades after the game, UCLA Coach Terry Donahue aban-

doned his usual understatement. "I thought our team played as well as we could have possibly wanted to play. We were awfully good tonight!"

They were, as they had been for five straight Rose Bowl victories, the winningest underdogs . . . or did they ever really believe they were the underdogs?

1987: EASTWARD HO!

After moving steadily westward for two decades, the balance of power in the Bowl shifted slightly to the East in 1987. No, it was not a resurgence of the once-dominant Big Ten, but the first Rose Bowl visit of the newest, and easternmost, Pac-10 team. Arizona State University, a member of the conference since 1978, beat the University of Michigan, 22-15, in their first trip to Pasadena.

ASU's inaugural success was not a complete surprise. Although they are not well-known in the East—partly because their home games are played at night, finishing up at midnight Central time or 1:00 Eastern, too late to meet most reporters' deadlines for the well-read Sunday morning sports sections—the

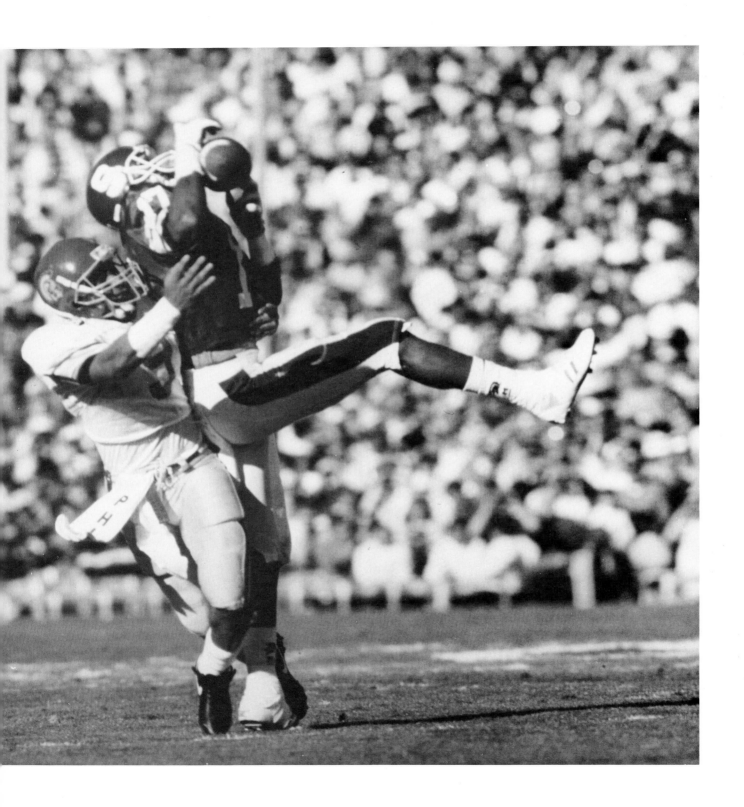

Sun Devils have had an impressive record in the West. By 1986 they had gone 5-2 against football powerhouse USC, 1-0 against Oklahoma, and 1-0 against Nebraska. In 1982 and 1985 they came frustratingly close to winning the Bowl bid. When they finally did it, they could credit their coach of two years, John Cooper, a ferocious offensive line, including All-American 293-pound tackle Danny Villa and 261-pound Randall McDaniel, and their quarterback Jeff Van Raaphorst.

Van Raaphorst's father, Richard, had been a placekicker on the 1961 Ohio State team that *should* have gone to the Bowl (staying at home in Columbus only because of a faculty veto). Jeff knew of his father's extreme disappointment and he had it in mind when he chose to play football at a Pac-10 school. He had promised his dad, and himself, that he would go to the Rose Bowl someday.

He went, saw, conquered, and came back with the award for the Player of the Game. He completed 16 of 30 passes for 193 yards and two touchdowns. None of the throws were bombs—the farthest one flew only 22 yards—but his passing was smooth and accurate, and Michigan never had the chance to intercept. Van Raaphorst was also willing to pass at risky, unpredictable moments. In the third quarter when the Wolverines were still leading, 15-13, the Sun Devils had the ball on the Michigan one yard-line. It was second down and the obvious ASU move would be to keep the ball on the ground. They did not have far to go, there was little danger of turning over the ball, and if they failed they could try again on the next down. But instead, Van Raaphorst passed to flanker Bruce Hill in the back of the end zone, and ASU had their second touchdown, putting them in the lead, 19-15.

The rest of the half, Arizona State simply looked faster and wilier than their foes. Jim Harbaugh, the Wolverines' star quarterback, after leading his team to two touchdowns in the first half, finished the game with only 13 completions out of 23 attempts. Twice he was sacked and three of his passes were intercepted. Wolverine tailback Jamie Morris, who had rushed for 1,039 yards during the season, tallied only 47 yards against ASU, 40 of them in the first half. After the humiliating loss, Bo Schembechler referred to the distracting ASU crowd noises and the grass as contributing to Michigan's loss. "It always appears when we're playing on artificial surfaces and they're playing on grass as if our speed is the same, but as soon as we both get on grass then it seems we're a step slower." Yet in his seventh Rose Bowl loss,

Opposite and following pages: Michigan State narrowly beat USC in the 1988 game, 23-20. Michigan State's Percy Snow was Player of the Game, and MSU's coach George Perles bested his opposite, Larry Smith in the latter's first season as USC's coach.

249

Schembechler seemed miffed when reporters asked why he (and the Big Ten) kept losing.

"You'll have to judge for yourselves," he said bitterly. "And I'm sure you'll have fun doing it." On the contrary, no one had much fun trying to explain why one of the winningest college football coaches of all time could have such bad luck in the Bowl.

But for Bo Schembechler and Michigan there is always next year. Whether a coach wins or loses, there is always hope. Whether a team is sporting shiny new Rose Bowl watches from their recent trip to Pasadena or whether they are like Oregon, which has not been there since 1958, or Northwestern, which has only been in the Bowl once, in 1948—every Pac-10 and Big Ten football player can hope that next year *he* will play in the Arroyo. "Every year you have a freshman class," says Northwestern athletic director Doug Single. "Every year you have new players who expect to get to the Rose Bowl." Every year when West meets Midwest the Bowl is up for grabs.

ROSE BOWL SCORES (since 1947)

1947	Illinois (7-2) Ray Eliot	**45**
	UCLA (10-0) Bert LaBrucherie	**14**
1948	Michigan (9-0) Fritz Crisler	**49**
	USC (7-1-1) Jeff Cravath	**0**
1949	Northwestern (7-2) Bob Voights	**20**
	California (10-0) Lynn "Pappy" Waldorf..	**14**
1950	Ohio State (6-1-2) Wes Fesler...........	**17**
	California (10-0) Lynn "Pappy" Waldorf..	**14**
1951	Michigan (5-3-1) Bennie Oosterbaan	**14**
	California (9-0-1) Lynn "Pappy" Waldorf .	**6**
1952	Illinois (8-0-1) Ray Eliot	**40**
	Stanford (9-1) Charles Taylor...........	**7**
1953	USC (9-1) Jess Hill	**7**
	Wisconsin (6-2-1) Ivan Williamson.......	**0**
1954	Michigan State (8-1) Clarence Munn.....	**28**
	UCLA (8-1) Henry "Red" Sanders........	**20**
1955	Ohio State (9-0) Woody Hayes...........	**20**
	USC (8-3) Jess Hill	**7**
1956	Michigan State (8-1) Duffy Daugherty ...	**17**
	UCLA (9-1) Henry "Red" Sanders........	**14**
1957	Iowa (8-1) Forest Evashevski	**35**
	Oregon State (7-2-1) Tommy Prothro	**19**
1958	Ohio State (8-1) Woody Hayes...........	**10**
	Oregon (7-3) Len Casanova.............	**7**
1959	Iowa (7-1-1) Forest Evashevski	**38**
	California (7-3) Pete Elliott.............	**12**
1960	Washington (9-1) Jim Owens	**44**
	Wisconsin (7-2) Milt Bruhn	**8**
1961	Washington (9-1) Jim Owens	**17**
	Minnesota (8-1) Murray Warmath	**7**
1962	Minnesota (7-2) Murray Warmath	**21**
	UCLA (7-3) Bill Barnes	**3**
1963	USC (10-0) John McKay.................	**42**
	Wisconsin (8-1) Milt Bruhn	**37**
1964	Illinois (7-1-1) Pete Elliott..............	**17**
	Washington (6-4) Jim Owens	**7**
1965	Michigan (8-1) Bump Elliott	**34**
	Oregon State (8-2) Tommy Prothro	**7**
1966	UCLA (7-2-1) Tommy Prothro	**14**
	Michigan State (10-0) Duffy Daugherty ..	**12**
1967	Purdue (8-2) Jack Mollenkopf	**14**
	USC (7-3) John McKay.................	**13**

1968	USC (9-1) John McKay..................	**14**
	Indiana (9-1) John Pont	**3**
1969	Ohio State (9-0) Woody Hayes...........	**27**
	USC (9-0-1) John McKay	**16**
1970	USC (9-0-1) John McKay	**10**
	Michigan (8-2) Bo Schembechler	**3**
1971	Stanford (8-3) John Ralston	**27**
	Ohio State (9-0) Woody Hayes..........	**17**
1972	Stanford (8-3) John Ralston	**13**
	Michigan (11-0) Bo Schembechler	**12**
1973	USC (11-0) John McKay.................	**42**
	Ohio State (9-1) Woody Hayes..........	**17**
1974	Ohio State (9-0-1) Woody Hayes	**42**
	USC (9-1-1) John McKay	**21**
1975	USC (10-1) John McKay.................	**18**
	Ohio State (10-1) Woody Hayes..........	**17**
1976	UCLA (8-2-1) Dick Vermeil	**23**
	Ohio State (11-0) Woody Hayes..........	**10**
1977	USC (10-1) John Robinson	**14**
	Michigan (10-1) Bo Schembechler	**6**
1978	Washington (7-4) Don James	**27**
	Michigan (10-1) Bo Schembechler	**20**
1979	USC (11-1) John Robinson	**17**
	Michigan (10-1) Bo Schembechler	**10**
1980	USC (10-0-1) John Robinson............	**17**
	Ohio State (11-0) Earle Bruce	**16**
1981	Michigan (9-2) Bo Schembechler	**23**
	Washington (9-2) Don James	**6**
1982	Washington (9-2) Don James	**28**
	Iowa (8-3) Hayden Fry	**0**
1983	UCLA (9-1-1) Terry Donahue	**24**
	Michigan (8-3) Bo Schembechler	**14**
1984	UCLA (7-4-1) Terry Donahue	**45**
	Illinois (10-2) Mike White	**9**
1985	USC (8-3) Ted Tollner	**20**
	Ohio State (9-2) Earle Bruce	**17**
1986	UCLA (9-2-1) Terry Donahue	**45**
	Iowa (10-2) Hayden Fry	**28**
1987	Arizona State (10-1) John Cooper	**25**
	Michigan (11-1) Bo Schembechler	**15**
1988	Michigan State George Perles	**23**
	USC Larry Smith	**20**

253

PHOTO CREDITS

All photographs, with the exception of those listed below, are courtesy of the Pasadena Tournament of Roses. Photographers: A. E. ARNOLD, MALCOLM W. EMMONS, MICHAEL GILL, GREG HARBAUGH, J. ALLEN HAWKINS, CLEM INSKEEP, BOB LONG, GEORGE LONG, TIM LONG, NORMAN MAUSKOPF, MARK ROGERS, DAVID STRADAL, PATRICIA TRYFORDS.

GEORGE LONG/SPORTS ILLUSTRATED: p. 221

RICHARD MACKSON/SPORTS ILLUSTRATED: p. 230

NATIONAL FOOTBALL FOUNDATION COLLEGE HALL OF FAME: p. 221

PASADENA HISTORICAL SOCIETY: pp. 22 bottom, 24 bottom, 25 bottom, 28

UPI/BETTMANN NEWSPHOTOS: pp. 180, 186, 187 right, 189, 192, 193, 194, 196 top and bottom, 252